PRAISES FOR
AFTER THE REUNION

"I really enjoyed *After the Reunion* and its emotional honesty. That feeling of trying to care for an elderly relative but needing to respect their wishes is so familiar for many people." **~Phoebe Shanahan, MA in English Literature**

"In *After the Reunion*, I find the heroines, who is the author, very remarkable. Really, truly and undeniable. Her strength, tenacity and perseverance are a lesson by themselves." **~Dimitra Manda, BA in English Language and Literature, English Teacher**

"Readers are waiting for this one. This is the book in which the author's mother opens up more. I like that the author was able to learn more about her mother." **~Ana Wells, Raymore, MO**

"This book is very well-written. It flows well…a good read."
~Kristen Driskill, Belton, MO

During the time period of this story, the author learned the diagnosis of her mother's mental illness. However, while she shared her symptoms, she made a personal decision not to share the actual diagnosis.

Dr. Grace LaJoy Henderson

AFTER THE REUNION

A Story of Acceptance

Inspirations by Grace LaJoy
Raymore, MO 64083

AFTER THE REUNION: A STORY OF ACCEPTANCE
Grace LaJoy Henderson

Disclaimer. I have tried to recreate events, locales and conversations from my memories of them. In order to maintain their anonymity in some instances I have changed the names of individuals and places. I may have changed some identifying characteristics and details such as physical properties, occupations and places of residence.

Due to the delicate subject of mental illness, all names are fictitious. I have taken great precaution to ensure my mother could not be located, while still sharing my real-life story.

Mission. Sharing my story to help increase awareness of mental illness.

Goal. Reducing stigma. Fostering connection. Inspiring hope.

AFTER THE REUNION: A STORY OF ACCEPTANCE
Copyright 2020. Grace LaJoy Henderson
Written by Grace LaJoy Henderson
Published by Inspirations by Grace LaJoy
Raymore, MO 64083

ISBN: 978-1-7341868-5-7

Printed in the United States of America

DEDICATION

To my daughter Arica. Thank you for traveling with me on that second visit to my mother. Your insight in helping me to communicate with her was awesome.

To my mother, "Geneva." Thank you for welcoming Arica and I when we came to visit you. I enjoyed listening as you recalled memories from your childhood and our family.

To the boarding home and behavioral health staff. Thank you for being so helpful and understanding. Your support, to my mother and us, was invaluable.

ACKNOWLEDGEMENT

The *Finding Mother Series* is my own recollection of my siblings' and my reunion with our mother after forty-nine years. When referring to my father, mother and siblings, I use fictitious names, as this is *my* story to tell. Their accounts may be different, as they may have perceived things from a different angle.

ABOUT THE SERIES

The *Finding Mother Series* is a complex, touching opportunity for readers to see into the author's journey to find her mother after decades. This series would be ideal for students at a secondary level who are searching for insight about the emotional conflicts and battles one must face when someone they care about has a mental illness. The four books in the series are segmented to provide specific lenses to the overall process, with a number of opportunities available for opening discussions about mental illness from both the author's point of view and her mother's.
~Leslie Arambula, MA Creative Writing, English Teacher

A WORD FROM THE AUTHOR

ABOUT THE FINDING MOTHER SERIES

Stories like mine are common and there is a sincere need to establish dialogue concerning this issue.

When I asked my mother how she felt about me publishing our reunion story, she laughed and said, "I guess it will be alright." Then she laughed again. She seemed flattered. Therefore, I really want her to feel proud about the way I present my recollection of the story. I told her I would not be revealing her real name or location.

To protect my mother's privacy, I have not revealed the full name under which she was found. I would never have found her under the name listed in my original foster care storybook. I believe that my personal recollection of our reunion details will inspire you. I hope it will decrease the stigma of mental illness in order to promote helpful discussion about this subject.

Due to my own personal struggle with the stigma surrounding mental illness, initially, I was only going to share the positive details of finding and reuniting with my mother. I did not intend to share any of the parts that were embarrassing for me. However, when others heard my story of how I found my mother after five decades, they told me they felt inspired. Many had similar stories. Realizing my personal story was intriguing, and could be helpful to so many people, I am sharing it…all of it.

AFTER THE REUNION: A STORY OF ACCEPTANCE
Grace LaJoy Henderson

TABLE OF CONTENTS

AFTER THE REUNION: A STORY OF ACCEPTANCE
Grace LaJoy Henderson

FOREWORD

As a little girl, knowing my mother's story, I felt sad that another child would grow up without a mother to take care of them.

Growing up, I observed closely every attempt my mother made to find Geneva. She even bought a book to learn how to be her own Private Investigator. Fueled by my mother's determination, I thought for certain that she would finally find her mother. Then after a failure too many, I would admit, "My mother will never find Geneva." All hope was lost. If Geneva were alive, we would have found a clue by now.

The day that my mother found Geneva I thought, "Finally, some good news!" I did not feel emotionally connected to my newly found grandmother. To me, my only grandmother was my father's mother. But, I was elated on my mother's behalf. She had spent the better part of her life searching for her. So, I hoped this would finally fill the void in her heart.

During the reunion, my mother called me after her first meeting with Geneva. Upon hearing that it was not going well, I felt a numbness. Thinking of my mother and uncles, I was disheartened. "She is going to hurt her children all over again, abandoning them for a second time."

The next day, I learned things were better. Happiness ensued. But, I could not understand why she acted the way she did the day before.

I went with my mother on her second visit to Geneva. The first time I met her, I realized the seriousness of her illness. Finally, I understood. I only hoped my mother would finally get the answers she deserved.

The *Finding Mother Series* will inspire readers to *feel* their feelings. It stirs people in similar situations to be at peace, but at the same time seek growth, in the midst of their circumstances.

~**Arica Miller, LMSW,**
School Social Worker
Daughter of the author

INTRODUCTION

When I returned home after our very emotional reunion with our long-lost mother, there were *two* things I deeply desired: to learn why she had left, by hearing her talk about her side of the story, and to inspire her to move to Kansas City so my brothers and I could take care of her.

I experienced an array of feelings and emotions. I called my mother often and we would talk on the phone for many minutes. However, whenever the subject came up of why she left our family, she would either start talking about something else, or tell me about the things she was hearing from the "people on the third floor."

Likewise, whenever I tried to discuss her moving to Kansas City, so we could take care of her, she would say she had business to take care of before she could move. She would also say she could not talk about it because the boarding home workers were always listening to her phone conversations, and she did not want them to know what we were saying.

When I asked her if I could help her take care of her business, she said she could do it herself. When I reminded her of how I had always wanted to find her and take care of her, she said she takes care of herself. Eventually, I began to wonder if she really had "business," or if she was just trying to protect my feelings because she did not know how to tell me that moving closer to us, and allowing us to take care of her, was never in her plans.

Seeing as she was avoiding the two things I really wanted to discuss, I used the next few weeks as an opportunity to get to know her better. I was able to learn about her personality and sense of humor. I learned what she liked and what she loved. I noticed she never mentioned things she did not like. I learned that she did not talk about negative memories, only positive ones. It appeared to me she had suppressed all of her hurtful memories. In addition to learning things about her, I was able to send her cards and gifts every once in a while.

I also used the next few weeks to search for assisted living centers in my area. Even though I highly doubted she would really consider moving, I wanted to be sure that Kansas City offered some options. I really wanted to find my mother a place equipped to care for her mental health needs. It was a bit of a shot in the dark, but I desired to be prepared just in case, by chance, she took our offer seriously and decided to move closer to us.

Three months later, my mother was still no closer to Kansas City – and I was still no closer to the answers I desired. I was overjoyed at finally being able to speak with her on the phone – something I had never dreamed possible. But, all of those years of wanting her in my life left me with a longing for answers that could only come from her. I realized I needed to make a second trip.

This time I took my adult daughter with me. My daughter's involvement was crucial in helping my mother feel comfortable enough to give me the answers I desperately needed.

I call this "a story of acceptance" because I ultimately had to accept my mother's responses to my two most pressing concerns. I also had to accept some other things that I learned about her.

Chapter 1

RETURNING HOME

AFTER THE REUNION

Besides still needing answers from my mother, when I returned home after the reunion, I continued to feel emotional. I also reached out again to Elsie, the caseworker at the Department of Children and Families, who had searched her database to see if my siblings were adopted through their agency.

A few days after the reunion, I took off work because I was not feeling well. While at home that day, I realized that part of the reason why I was not feeling well was because I was struggling with the way my mother was living.

I felt so downhearted that I sensed I needed someone trustworthy to talk to, to externalize my emotions. Because of the shock that came with finding my mother living in poverty, I had to be extra careful not to talk to just anyone. Most importantly I had to do it sooner rather than later.

After a meticulous online search, I found the number of a counseling hotline where I could speak with someone freely without revealing my true identity. When I called, a woman answered and I asked her if this was the type of line where I can have a counseling session with someone. She said it was not exactly counseling, but a line in which people talked and she listened. She said she could listen if I needed to talk.

Feeling like this was just what I needed, I asked, "So, I can start talking to you right now and you will listen?"

"Yes," she readily answered.

Realizing I finally had a golden opportunity to share what was on my heart concerning my mother, with someone who did not know me and therefore could not judge me, tears welled up in my eyes. I cried and began to talk about my feelings.

I talked about how I found my mother after forty-nine years, and how I was not happy about the place she has been living. I expressed how my mother was living with beggars and peddlers who steal from her. I conveyed how I had always imagined I would find her in a mental hospital, locked up, maybe drugged up and not able to speak. I thought she would be in a safe environment, unlike where she was. She was living in a place where she has to pray for her safety every single day.

My mother is not supposed to be living under those impoverished conditions.

I had never imagined she would actually be able to speak, nor that she would be living in such disadvantaged surroundings.

AFTER THE REUNION: A STORY OF ACCEPTANCE
Grace LaJoy Henderson

I told the woman that, over the years before finding my mother, I had often thought of starting a homeless shelter that would accommodate anyone and everyone who needed a place to live, with no requirements and no expectations. They could just come get their needs met, be it food, a warm, dry place to lay their head for one night or a permanent place of shelter. Whenever I had those thoughts, I never imagined my own mother would be living in a similar environment.

Fortunately, she was not homeless.

She had been there for over fifteen years, so even though I did not like where she was living, she was surrounded by a stable environment, which she was content to call her home. Accepting this, I began to feel better about my mother's situation.

A sense of appreciation came over me as I realized I had actually come an extremely long way from having no idea where my mother was to finally finding her and talking with her!

The woman on the counseling hotline sensed I was feeling better. She had done a great job keeping quiet, and simply listening, while I vented. However, my story had sparked her interest. She asked my permission to ask me a couple of questions about the reunion to satisfy her curiosity.

I said, "Sure!"

Her inquiry led to us conversing for another ten minutes after my emotions were content.

She admitted, "I am intrigued by your story. How did you finally find your mother?"

I told her, "It was a long, tedious journey, but I ultimately found her through an online people search."

"How did she feel about being found?" she asked.

I briefly told her the story of how, at first, she denied us then accepted us the next day after some prompting and prodding.

She said, "Wow! What a fascinating story!"

I felt impressed by her courage to ask me questions and I was happy to answer them. I appreciated her interest in my story.

I thanked her for listening to me and we said our good-byes. I hung up the phone feeling as if a very large weight had been taken away from me. With that burden lifted, I felt happy for the rest of the day and was able to return to work the next day feeling refreshed.

It was days after this "counseling" phone call that I began to spend more time on the phone with mother and sending her things.

Soon after that, I contacted Elsie again. Now that I had gotten my siblings names directly from my own mother, I remembered Elsie's generous offer. She had told me that if I ever learned my siblings' names, I should feel free to reach out to her again. I felt fortunate to know someone who had access to databases and was willing to help me anytime.

I emailed Elsie and told her I had finally found my mother after almost fifty years and that she was able to tell me the names of the children she had after leaving. I gave her the names and dates of birth for all four of the children and asked her if she would check to see if any of them were adopted through her agency. After I had sent the email, I sensed that with all the information I possessed that she was bound to find something this time. I felt very hopeful as I waited for her response.

Six days later, she emailed me back.

She was very excited that I had been reunited with my mother.

"Wow, that is amazing!! Hope it is going well as you two reconnect," she wrote, before thanking me for providing my siblings' information, and informing me that she would do everything in her power to help me. She said she would let me know the results of her search. I continued to feel hopeful as I anticipated what she would find.

While waiting for her response, I kept on trying to find an appropriate place for my mother to live, just in case, by chance, she actually decided to move to Kansas City to be closer to us.

AFTER THE REUNION: A STORY OF ACCEPTANCE
Grace LaJoy Henderson

Chapter 2

MY SEARCH FOR

A PLACE FOR MOTHER

After the remarkable reunion, I continued to process my feelings about the condition in which I had found my mother. She said she used to walk outside a lot but not so much anymore for fear of being harmed. Therefore, my desire to provide for her became even stronger.

You see, ever since I was a little girl, I had always dreamed of finding my mother and taking care of her. Before reuniting with her, as soon as I knew we had located her, I began to think about moving her from where she was to where we were. Especially after the boarding home office manager, April, had warned us, before the reunion that we were not going to be happy when we saw her living conditions.

My mother was in her eighties, and had not received any family support for many years. Therefore, I assumed she should be more than ready to come and be with us, and allow us to take care of her.

So, I began discussing with April the type of facility I should be looking for in Kansas City that would meet her needs before we even saw our mother for the first time after so many years.

She explained to me that Geneva resided in an assisted living facility, in which they cook, clean, wash clothes, and manage medication for the residents. She had said that if I found a similar place in Kansas City, it would be seamless to transfer her from their facility to the new one. She told me to be sure to search for places that would accept my mother's source of income.

Yes, April had given me all the information I needed to begin searching for assisted living for my mother before we even reunited with her.

After the reunion, I continued reviewing the benefits and amenities of numerous facilities. One of the first things I learned was that there is a difference between assisted living centers and nursing homes.

Assisted living centers cater to people who are able to take care of themselves, but who may need some assistance with daily living. Nursing homes cater to people who are not able to care for themselves, who need a higher level of care.

The assisted living facility where we found our mother is also known as a boarding home. One of the requirements for her to stay there was that she must attend *the center* daily, from early morning until late afternoon. "The center" is a mental health treatment center. All of the boarding home residents, including Geneva, receive transportation to and from there in a large blue bus every weekday.

The work of the center includes evaluating mental health patients, setting behavior goals, creating treatment plans and providing therapeutic activities. While there, Mother participates with group counseling, games and trips to the park. She also receives lunch and a snack and learns life skills.

In my search for an assisted living facility for her, a nurse told me that since she has a serious mental illness, she would also be eligible to live in a nursing home. However, my mother is very independent and when I visited nursing homes, the patients were severely handicapped and my mother is too independent to fit in with that environment. I ended up settling for two assisted living centers from which to choose. However, I was leaning more towards one in particular.

The first facility was located seventeen minutes away from my home and was set up like a large newer home. I liked that it was new and clean and that no more than twelve residents could live there at one time. An added plus to that was that all the rooms were located on one level. This would be ideal for my mother because she wouldn't have to climb stairs and strain her pained hip even more. As it happened, luck was on my side and they actually had two openings!

My mother would enjoy twenty-four-hour care, her own private room, and a private bathroom. She would also have meals prepared for her and someone to administer her medication daily. She could check out and go wherever she pleased. My first thought was that I could take her to places or even bring her to my home for visits if she wanted.

The second facility was located twenty-five minutes from my home and was an older building. It was very nice and clean, with a forty-residents limit. They actually had a couple of vacancies on the first floor. This facility had the same benefits as the other one, and then some more.

In addition to caretakers, it had a round-the-clock nurse, security, and a doctor who visits on site. My mother would have a psychiatrist who actually comes to her on location to monitor her mental illness and medications. She would even receive treatment and physical therapy for her hip right there on site!

The second facility also featured a chapel for Sunday morning worship, so my mother could attend if she wanted. There was a beauty salon, so she could have her hair washed and styled regularly. In addition, a full-service nursing home was attached to the assisted living home. Therefore, if my mother ever became unable to care for herself, she could move directly over to the nursing home without us having to find a new place for her to live. After visiting both places, I liked the second one best. I requested a packet of information to share with my brothers, with hopes of having an opportunity to share it with my mother during my second trip. That way she would see for herself how much we wanted her and that we would do anything to have her in our lives once again.

AFTER THE REUNION: A STORY OF ACCEPTANCE
Grace LaJoy Henderson

Chapter 3

A TYPICAL PHONE
CALL WITH MOTHER

As time passed, my phone calls with mother became more frequent. Initially, we would talk once a month, but after a short while, we would be on the phone every other week. Sometimes, we spoke again after only a few days. Mother was a regular thought in my mind so I was often thinking about what I could do for her, be it talking on the phone, mailing her a package, or researching living facilities.

Whenever we would talk on the phone and I would ask her if she needed anything, she always let me know what she needed. Whenever I sent her things, she was always happy to receive them. In fact, she would remind me of holidays that were coming up, which I liked.

The first time I called her after we got home from reuniting with her she told me, "You know Mother's Day is coming up on the 13th of May?" In a later phone conversation, she reminded me of her birthday and Christmas.

Almost a year later, when Valentine's Day was two weeks away, she said to me, "You know Valentine's Day is coming up?" When I told her that I sent her a Valentine's Day gift, she told me, "I love surprises!" Her reminders let me know what occasions were important to her, so, I made sure to send her gifts for each one of them.

When she would remind me of those special dates, I felt happy that she was comfortable doing so. It filled my heart with joy. I liked that she was able to open up with me and communicate exactly what was important to her. I also felt honored that she was willing to accept gifts from me. Overall, I felt pleased that she was mentally able to express herself in this way because this meant I did not have to go through the trouble of inquiring about what she wants and needs to the boarding home workers. It was my great pleasure to provide anything she desired.

Most of the time, our conversations were just random chatting. Whenever I would call and speak to her, the ritual would go like this:

"May I speak to Geneva?"

The boarding home worker would reply, "Just a moment. Geneva! Your daughter is on the phone! Somebody go tell Geneva her daughter is on the phone."

Then usually two to four minutes later a, now familiar, voice would inquire on the other side of the phone, "Hello?"

A huge smile would break up on my face before regaining my composure enough to say, "Hello, Mother, how are you doing?"

"Oh, so-so, my hip has been hurting."

Quite often she would ask questions like, "What have you been doing?" or "Did you do anything fun today?"

That would be the only urge I would need to tell her all about my day and my writing.

Each time, the topic varied, because the turn of our conversation would depend on her follow-up questions like, "Did you go to church today?" "Do you still go to Sunday School?" "Have you talked to Carla?" or "How is Terrance doing?"

When I called her on the Fourth of July, she asked me if my church was doing anything special that day.

I told her my church has never celebrated the Fourth of July.

She told me that when she was little girl, her church *always* celebrated *every* holiday, and that her church would have cookouts at the park. She often asked the same questions in our current conversation that she asked in our past conversations. I always enjoyed answering all of her questions.

It seemed she was asking me those questions for a few reasons. The first, she may have appreciated me calling her and she enjoyed talking to me. The second, she could have wanted me to feel like she really wanted to talk to me, especially since a lot of the time she would prefer to be in her bed resting her hip. A third, she might have been aiming towards being kind to her daughter whom she knew loved her.

Even with her mental illness, I believe she recognized that she could possibly sadden me if it appeared she did not want to be bothered with me. Remembering my responses to her questions was a sign, to me, that she enjoyed hearing them. I felt intrigued whenever she would inquire, in a later conversation, about something we discussed in a prior one.

During our phone conversations, I usually asked her if she had received any package that I may have sent, and if she liked it. She usually liked everything.

She would tell me about the weather in her city. She would say, "It is cold here!" or "It is hot like a furnace outside!"

Oftentimes, she would talk about the center that she attends daily, telling me what they served for lunch, which was usually something she really liked. She would inform me about the special meals, like when the center served Thanksgiving dinner, or the boarding home had a cookout and served barbecue for the Fourth of July.

Sometimes, when she would want to get off the phone, but wanted to avoid hurting my feelings, she pretended the boarding home workers needed to use the phone. I remember one time vividly.

We were in the middle of a conversation when Mother's voice went distant from the receiver and I heard her saying, "Do you need to call that lady who called earlier?"

I frowned down on my phone. "Mother, do you need to get off the phone?"

"I think so. You see, a woman called earlier and I think they want to call her back."

I was feeling torn between continuing our conversation and letting her go. "Do they need you to get off the phone?"

"No!" I heard one of the workers proclaim from the background. "Nobody needs to use the phone. She wants to get off the phone, but she is trying to blame us."

Mother released an embarrassing chuckle.

"Mother, they are telling on you."

"Yeah," she said, before letting out another quiet laugh.

In that moment, I experienced a series mixed thoughts.

Should I feel sad about her trying to be sneaky about getting off the phone? Does she not want to talk to me? If she needs to go, why don't she just say so?

"Mother, I can let you go. I like to call you every once in a while, to see how you are doing and to let you know I am thinking about you. You don't have to stay on the phone for a long time, unless you want to. Do you need to get off the phone?"

Mother humbly replied, "It's okay. So, what have you been doing?

Then after a few more words back and forth, she said, "Well, I want to go lay in my bed and rest a little."

I said, "Okay, it was very nice talking to you."

"It was nice talking to you, too."

"Have a nice rest of the day," I told her.

"Thank you. You, too."

"Okay, bye."

She said, "Bye."

After that call ended, memories flooded back of all of the other times when Mother did that same thing, but the workers never clearly told on her that way. She just succeeded in getting off the phone.

During our talks, I learned some fun facts about her. She loves cookies and banana pudding. She loves desserts in general. She enjoys telling stories about herself when she was growing up. When she was a little girl, she really enjoyed licking the cake and cookie batter out of the bowl after her mother would fill the baking pans.

Our conversations usually consisted of the same types of dialogue each time. I cannot say I blame her for preferring to be by herself rather than talking on the phone. After all, she had been to herself for many, many years, with no family. So, getting phone calls from her children was something new for her, something she had to get used to.

I actually felt disappointed and took it personally at the first indication that she did not feel like talking when I would call, especially since I truly desired for her to open up and tell me why she left us. Also, I really needed to know her true feelings about allowing us to move her to Kansas City. Therefore, a second trip to visit Mother became more and more appealing.

AFTER THE REUNION: A STORY OF ACCEPTANCE
Grace LaJoy Henderson

Chapter 4

MY SECOND TRIP TO VISIT MOTHER

The need for answers to my burning questions was so potent that I made a second trip to visit my mother. This time, I planned to take my daughter, Arica, with me. I needed a travel partner, and I thought this would be a great opportunity for her to meet her grandmother. Arica is a Licensed Social Worker and so her expertise came in handy during our trip in a way I never expected.

Leading up to my second trip, mother acted very excited about our coming. Whenever I would call her, she would ask, "Are you and Arica still coming? June 7th, right?" Every time one of my brothers called her, she would ask them, "Are Grace and Arica still coming on June 7th?" I felt happy about her being excited to see us and could not wait for her to meet Arica.

There were several things I wanted to do together during our trip and I discussed my expectations with my mother over the phone.

I asked her, "Would you allow me to take you out to dinner during our visit?"

She said, "Yeah. That would be okay."

"Also, I would like to show you some information about a couple of assisted living facilities that I have in mind for you. I understand you may never decide to move, but I just wanted to give you something tangible to think about."

She said, "Yeah. That would be okay, too."

I could not bottle up my final expectation any longer. I told her that when we are in person during our visit, that I wanted her to tell me why she left. I felt my breath catch in my throat and the moment her voice affirmed that it would be okay, I felt overwhelmed.

She agreed to all of my requests, so I felt increasingly excited about our visit and could not wait. Even though I knew she probably would not agree to move, I was extremely hopeful. I was even prepared to bring her back in the car with us if she agreed to it. Admittedly, my hopes were up way too high, but that did not stop me from remaining highly optimistic. I really wanted my mother to live closer to us. I often imagined how great it would be for her to be in Kansas City, to meet all of her grandchildren; and for all of us to throw a big dinner just to celebrate her.

Although I really wanted to bring my mother back to be closer to us, I knew I could not do it by myself. I needed my brothers' support that they so amply provided. When Arica and I were making our plans, my brother, Terrance, pitched in some cash to help us pay for the trip. Our hope was that I would use the trip to convince our mother to move to Kansas City. We really, really wanted her near us, to make her happy by providing for all of the things she needed and wanted. Our biggest hope was to be able to give her the life we felt she deserved. Therefore, this trip would not be just for fun and enjoyment. We were on a true mission!

As Arica and I continued to prepare for the trip, we decided we would drive a rental car. It would be a seventeen-hour drive, but we estimated that it would take us at least a day to get there, with all the stops for food and rest. We agreed on a hotel that was only a ten-minute drive from the boarding home where my mother lived. The hotel we chose provided free continental breakfast so that would save us some time and money.

While packing, I started thinking about our prior visit when we reunited with Mother. I remembered the great effect that the family photos I had taken with me had on her ability to recall memories of her life before leaving us so many years earlier. I remembered the sincere interest she had shown in the photos and how much she had enjoyed them.

During our reunion visit, I noted that the more she looked at the pictures, the more it began to "click" for her that we were her children. The more she realized we were her children, the more she opened up, and eventually accepted us. To say that the pictures were a powerful tool would be an understatement. However, during our initial reunion visit, I had run out of pictures to show her and I wished I had brought more.

For this second trip Arica and I were preparing for, I sorted through my many albums, pulled out as many photos as I thought she would appreciate and packed them up. I even took a little album, full of pictures of herself and her adopted family, that our cousin had given me to show her. Our cousin believed that those pictures would help jog her memory.

I was thrilled to be able to take so many because I knew she didn't have any. With all the moving around, and her health being such as it is she had lost every tangible memory of her family.

Initially, we had planned to leave on the morning of Thursday, June 8th. However, the rental car company informed us that we could pick the car up after five o'clock the evening before without any additional fee. That opportunity moved things forward and we decided to take advantage of it and get on the road that very evening. My brother, Jerome, was concerned, because he didn't like the idea of our having to drive through the night on unfamiliar roads.

He urged us to leave early the next morning so that our travel would be mostly daytime hours. Even though I understood his concern, the thought of getting on the road as soon as possible appealed to me. I felt like the sooner we were on our way the sooner we would reach our destination. Arica and I discussed it, and she was all for getting a head start. We packed our suitcases and plenty of healthy snacks, picked up our rental car, and drove straight to the highway!

One of the most remarkable things about our twenty-four-hour road trip was that my oldest brother, Jerome, contacted us every so often to make sure we were safe. He encouraged us not to sleep in the car at rest stops, but to book a hotel instead.

As the main driver, I was perfectly capable of functioning with only a few hours of sleep, so checking into a hotel seemed excessive to me. In the end, Arica and I decided to chance it and slept in the car in well-lit large convenient store parking lots, whenever we stopped to get gas. Each time after we would wake up, I bought a cup of coffee to help me keep awake until the next time we would stop. Even though we did not do as my brother suggested, his phone calls and texts were very welcomed. I felt like he really cared about us, and that alone was the only sense of security I needed.

During the trip, Arica and I talked, laughed and listened to music. I was happy because that was a chance to bond with my daughter. A special opportunity to spend time together.

My most memorable experience, during our drive there, was enjoying the variety of healthy snacks that Arica prepared.

AFTER THE REUNION: A STORY OF ACCEPTANCE
Grace LaJoy Henderson

She had brought along several soft, perfectly ripe avocados and a loaf of fresh bread.

On one of our stops along the way, she peeled and removed the seeds from three or four of the avocados, put the edible portion in a clear glass bowl and mashed it with a fork.

She added salt and pepper and stirred to her desired consistency. Then took a slice of bread in one hand and a fork in the other. My daughter dipped the fork into the bowl, which sat on her lap atop of the blanket and pillow that was keeping her warm and comfortable throughout the drive.

When she had just the right portion of the avocado mixture on the fork, she spread it on to the slice of bread.

I watched intensely as she completed the task.

As I stared, she stretched her arm towards me with the prepared avocado snack sitting on her hand. "This one is for you," she said.

I felt honored and joyful to receive it. My daughter's avocado bread had always been one of my favorite finger foods.

Then she made one for herself.

As I was biting into the delicious snack that my daughter had so carefully prepared, I thought about how grateful I felt that finding my mother had resulted in my sharing this special moment together with my daughter.

AFTER THE REUNION: A STORY OF ACCEPTANCE
Grace LaJoy Henderson

Several times we stopped for gas, food, and to get some rest. We enjoyed our journey, taking our time and not being in a rush. We were careful to stay within the speed limit throughout the entire trip, until finally reaching our destination. I did most of the driving but as we got closer, Arica took the wheel and drove us the final way. After we got off the highway in my mother's city, traffic was very congested.

I felt relieved to finally arrive, but I felt nervous in the high-volume traffic.

The people who were driving on the road around us seemed unconcerned about other drivers or common safety rules. Whenever we had the right of way, the other drivers did not yield to allow us to have it. Driving in that city was clearly different from Kansas City. In the end, we just allowed everyone to pass us by because it would earn us nothing but a headache, not to mention that it would sour our anticipation and good mood.

It had been twenty-four hours since we had started our trip, and now we were weaving our rental car through the somewhat familiar roads leading to our hotel. I felt relieved as we entered the parking lot, walked into the hotel and strolled over to the front desk to check in. This meant we were that much closer to finally spending time with my mother.

AFTER THE REUNION: A STORY OF ACCEPTANCE
Grace LaJoy Henderson

Chapter 5

ARRIVING ON THURSDAY EVENING

It was around five o'clock in the evening of June 7th when we left Kansas City; and it was around five o'clock in the evening of June 8th when we arrived at our out-of-town hotel. Arica and I were both tired and felt like resting, but I was too excited and wanted to go see my mother right away.

The anticipation of driving to the boarding home where she lived was intense. The thought of getting back into the car and driving on the hectic roads was not appealing to me, though.

The last time I went to the boarding home, I was with my brothers, but this time, I was going to be with my daughter. I was concerned about returning to that rundown and unkempt neighborhood without the company of strong men. Would we feel safe?

Would Arica and I be able to sit inside long enough to truly enjoy our visit with the foul odor that seemed to fill every corner of that boarding home?

Even with those concerns, this was my mother and she was worth any inconvenience that I would experience just to see her, talk to her, and finally get the answers to my two pressing concerns.

I knew my mother did not know the exact time we were coming. I had called the boarding home several times but either the line stayed busy or no one answered the phone. Therefore, I had no other way of letting my mother know when to expect us. I knew she had been excited about us coming. I just hoped she would be prepared for our visit when we showed up.

After we had settled in at the hotel, we freshened up and left to go see my mother. Twenty minutes later, my daughter and I entered the building. In my hands, I was clutching the small bag containing all the photos I had so meticulously collected.

After taking a moment to adjust to the odor, we headed for the office. We told the worker we were there to see my mother, Geneva. She sent one of the residents to get her.

While waiting for Mother to enter the room, I asked, "Is April here? She is the person who I spoke to on the phone when I finally located my mother after so many years, and I have wished to meet her in person." The worker responded, "I am sorry, she is not here. She will not be back into the office again until next week." Feeling a sense of disappointment, I knew meeting April was not something that was going to happen during this trip.

When my mother came to greet us, she had a big smile on her face and seemed very happy to see us. She was carrying a very large black backpack in one of her hands. I immediately remembered that the last time I visited her, she was carrying around two plastic grocery bags. By the looks of it, she had graduated to a backpack and it appeared she was carrying around a lot more stuff now than what she had toted in the bags.

I wondered if it was because I had been sending her things, so now she had more belongings to carry around. She told us during our first visit that when she leaves things in her bedroom, other residents steal it. She really enjoyed receiving things from me and my brothers. Although I liked sending her things, I carried some guilt about the fact she had to carry it everywhere she went. I felt sad because the more I sent, the more she had to carry around. It was simply wrong. That was not how things were supposed to be for a person in her state and age.

That was yet another thing that sparked my already strong desire to take her out of that place and move her to Kansas City. She would be so much better in a safe facility where she could leave her stuff in her room without the fear of it being stolen.

After going in for a great big hug and a kiss on Mother's cheek, I took one tiny step back, and looked at the beautiful young lady that had traveled with me.

"This is my daughter, Arica, your Granddaughter!" I said to Geneva with a proud-like excitement. Gleaming, she looked at

43

Arica's face, then, looked at my face, as if to see there was any resemblance.

Arica fixed her eyes on Mother's face. "Wow, it is wonderful to finally meet you!"

"It is nice to meet you, too," Mother smiled.

"It is amazing how much my mother favors you."

They both were smiling.

It gave me a feeling of sheer gratefulness to finally have the honor of introducing them.

She invited us to sit in the large living room area. The living room featured brown hardwood floors, an old non-functional fireplace, a large television mounted on the wall, two long couches, and some chairs.

The couches were dirty. The odor was unbearable, yet familiar. It filled the home during our initial reunion visit. But, we all were so caught up with the tension of the reunion that the odor seemed insignificant. Smelling it at the second visit made me feel saddened because I was thinking we could provide her a much better living environment, if only she would accept our offer.

Overall, the living room was organized, the walls were free of flaws, and the floor was clean.

There was a door in the living room that led to the office area. The top half of the office door was opened while the bottom half remained shut. I presumed this was to keep boarding home residents from entering the office. I saw a worker in there.

The television was on, turned up loud and showing a movie. About four or five residents were sitting in the living room watching it. My mother, Arica and I did not really talk about anything significant since the noise prevented us from having a meaningful conversation. However, I showed my mother some of the pictures I had brought and she seemed to be enjoying them very much. Her interest was especially piqued by the ones of my oldest sister, Carla, and those of herself when she was a little girl.

During our first reunion visit, I had given her my only copy of an Army picture of my sister, Danisha. When I went back home, I wished I had taken a copy of the picture with my cell phone. So, now that I was in person with my mother again, I asked her if she still had the picture and if it would be possible for me to snap a photo on my mobile phone.

"Yes," was all she answered and she stood up and left the living room, heading for the direction of her bedroom.

While she was gone, I kept looking towards the direction she went, watching for her return. Five minutes later, the familiar feeling of abandonment consumed me and I feared she wouldn't be coming back. Lifting myself off the couch, I went to her room and knocked lightly on the locked door. As I was waiting for her to open, I had an awful feeling, like she was never going to open it.

Finally, she opened the door and came out of the room with the picture in hand. I was relieved, as the few moments that I waited outside of the door seemed like an hour. She looked at me as if to wonder why I could not wait.

Suddenly, I felt embarrassed for my irrational feelings, but mostly surprised by my reaction. I was wondering what had come over me because normally I would have been able to wait with no problem. I was afraid she might be offended by my inability to wait for her to return. However, seeing the considerate look on her face, it was like she actually understood. We went back into the living room and sat on the couch with Arica.

As my mother continued to enjoy the pictures, I was still dwelling on how I had experienced fear that my mother was not going to come back when she went to her bedroom to get the picture. I was wondering if I had reverted back to the two-year-old abandoned toddler who wanted her mother to come back, but she never returned. I wondered if what I was experiencing was a fear of being abandoned by my mother for a second time.

In analyzing the situation, I recalled three instances when I was three and four years old, and felt afraid of being abandoned by my grandmother. She babysat me while my father worked after my mother had left.

AFTER THE REUNION: A STORY OF ACCEPTANCE
Grace LaJoy Henderson

The first instance was when my grandmother took me to her niece's house to leave me while she ran some errands. I refused to go to her niece because I had this notion that if I went to her, my grandmother would walk out and never come back.

The second instance was when my grandmother took me to a daycare center to leave me there for a few hours. Once again, the exact same thing happened. I refused to go with the daycare worker for fear of never seeing my grandmother again.

The last incidence was when grandmother led me to the kindergarten for the first time. I remember being terrified that if I would turn my back and sit down with the rest of the children, she would leave and never return.

In each of those instances, I witnessed my grandmother hesitating to leave, by hiding behind walls and peeping around corners until I was finally distracted enough for her to sneak away.

I finally finished analyzing that awkward situation and brought my thoughts back into the current moment. I noticed my mother was looking closely at one of the pictures from the album my cousin had sent. It was a picture of her standing in front of her childhood home. She quoted the address and stared at that picture much longer than any of the other ones.

Intrigued by the way she was gazing at the photo, I asked her what it was about that picture that she could not take her eyes off it.

"That's me!" she said.

I felt surprised that of all the pictures I had shown her of herself, she liked that one the most. That one was not a close-up like some of the other ones, nor were her facial features as clear. Nevertheless, that one captured her heart.

As she continued to look at the small photo album, she recognized a picture of my grandmother's husband.

"That looks like my uncle who raised me," she said.

I told her that was him. Then she grinned as she talked about how she used to comb his hair, when he had hair. He had a bald head in the picture. Since she was enjoying the pictures in that album more than I expected, I told her she could keep the entire album. My cousin predicted those pictures would jog her memory and she was right!

After the high I was feeling while watching her enjoying herself with those pictures, a calm nervousness engulfed me. We were having such a great time, but I suddenly remembered my main reasons for being there.

It dawned on me that I was sitting right beside the woman who I needed answers from. I felt like it was now or never. I was thinking that when we took her out to dinner, I would ask her to tell me her story about why she had left. That would be the right way to pursue the issue since I believed she would be able to talk freely away from the prying ears of her housemates.

Therefore, I used this moment to seek her true intentions about moving to Kansas City.

I asked her if she had thought any more about moving to live closer to us. She looked over at the office area as if she could not answer because the office workers would be nosey and listen to our conversation.

She said, "I can't talk here."

I asked her if she wanted to go into another room or outside.

I told her I really needed to know and would respect whatever her answer may be. Understanding this, she told me that when she first moved into the boarding home, fifteen years ago, it was in way worse condition.

She said they had done many nice things to the house, like fixing major holes in the walls and painting. She explained that she was used to being there. Furthermore, she expressed that she did not want to leave at this time.

Although I was saddened, I understood how she felt, and most of all, I truly appreciated her honesty.

I knew I had a packet full of assisted living information out in the car, but was afraid to show it to her since we obviously would not be bringing her to live in Kansas City anytime soon.

My brother Terrance and I had discussed leaving the information with her so she would at least have something tangible to look at and think about. However, my optimism had faded and I felt afraid to mention it to her after she had made her intentions clear. I said nothing about it and let it stay in the car.

My daughter and I saw that it was getting dark outside. We had planned on going to a restaurant for dinner before it got too late. I asked my mother if it was okay for us to visit her at the center the next day.

She said, "Yes. Nobody has ever visited me there before, but that will be okay." She told us that Friday would be finger nail polish day.

We hugged, said our good-byes, and returned to our hotel.

That night, I spoke with Terrance on the phone to get his opinion about whether I should have shown our mother the assisted living information, since she had clearly indicated not wanting to move.

He insisted that I *should* have and instructed me to leave it with her so she could at least have something tangible to contemplate. Since we sacrificed the time and resources to travel all the way there just for the opportunity to try to convince her, we could not give up now. Besides me wanting to talk to her about why she left, the entire purpose of the visit was to try to win her over to bring her to Kansas City.

This was our only shot at giving her the information. We knew that once I was back home, it would be impossible to have that type of discussion with her. We had to take advantage of the up close and personal opportunity that I had with her while I was there.

Based on Terrance's counsel, I planned to take the information and talk with her about it when we visited her the next day. We ended our conversation.

Arica and I shared our thoughts about how the evening had gone before we retired to our beds for a good night's sleep. As I dozed off that night, I felt like we had a great time with my mother. I truly enjoyed the first day of our visit and I could not wait to wake up to the second.

AFTER THE REUNION: A STORY OF ACCEPTANCE
Grace LaJoy Henderson

Chapter 6

DAY TWO OF OUR VISIT - FRIDAY

I woke up the next morning, envisioning the fun we would have sitting in the center, participating in activities with my mother. Then I started thinking about the two specific purposes I had for going back again to visit my mother. I would wait until Sunday to ask her about why she left her family so many years ago. I longed to know her story.

However, today, I knew that I had to show her the assisted living information that I brought. I knew I would need to leave it with her so that she could have something to ponder over after we left. I was feeling grateful for Terrance inspiring me to go ahead and give her the packet of information.

My mother had told Arica and I to come to the center around noon. So, we ate an early lunch at a downtown restaurant before going. When we arrived at the address, we met the center manager, Donna, outside as we approached the door of the building. She asked if she could help us find something. I told her we were looking for the center. She told us we were at the right place, but seemed puzzled about what we were doing there. After all, most of the people who attend the center do not have families or visitors.

I told her I was Geneva's daughter and that my siblings and I had found her after forty-nine years.

She expressed a variety of feelings.

"Oh my, I am so excited that the two of you are here! This is a surprise! I never even knew Geneva *had* children! It is amazing that you were able to find your long-lost loved one after so many years."

She graciously invited us into the building. We walked up two flights of stairs to arrive at the front door of the center. As we stood outside of the that door, Donna was still in shock that we were actually there.

"I am so delighted that you all came! Most of the mental health patients who attend our center do not have anyone who cares about them. So, we are *always* in support of families who are concerned and want to be involved."

I told her of my desire to move my mother to Kansas City to be closer to us, and of my intent to try to woo her into considering it.

She said she would do anything in her power to help my siblings and me. Then, she gave me her cellular phone number and told me I was welcome to call her anytime. She told me that her and my mother joked around with each other a lot, but she did not really know a lot about her personal life because my mother tends to be private.

She also told me my mother had a mental illness and that, as long as she took her medication, she was nice and did not bother anyone. She mentioned they recently had some difficulty getting her to take it consistently. She told me a story of how the workers noticed she had been acting angry and cussing at people more than usual.

The staff came up with a bright idea to check under the mattress on her bed. There they found the pills she was supposed to be taking daily, but she had been hiding them instead. Donna said she had to remind my mother that if she did not take her medication that she could end up locked up in a mental hospital again. Having a fear of going back there, she started taking it regularly.

There seemed to be a consensus among all of the workers that she "was nice, quiet, and does not bother anybody." Donna said the thing that impressed her the most about Geneva is she resides around drugs all day, every day in the boarding home, but she will not touch them.

I felt very amazed and grateful to hear that my mother had no interest in using drugs.

I told her I was looking forward to joining my mother in the center activities. However, she explained that the center was a mental health treatment center. Therefore, to maintain the privacy of the patients, outsiders were not allowed to enter. I felt a little let down and kind of embarrassed for expecting to participate, not knowing it was private. She invited us to sit down in the lobby area while she went in to get Geneva.

With her backpack in hand, Geneva came walking out, with a cheerful grin on her face. She sat down in a chair. She seemed very happy that we were there.

For a moment, I was feeling a little guilt, like we were causing her to miss the center activities. Then I realized the staff probably felt like visiting with her long-lost family may be more therapeutic to her than participating with the center for that day. Besides, she goes to the center every day, but it is rare for family to visit.

Just then, Donna came out of the center door with a very happy-for-Geneva type of look on her face and asked, "Geneva, who are these people?"

Not realizing we had already told Donna who we were, my mother told her that it was none of her business.

Donna asked, "Is this your daughter and your granddaughter?"

My mother looked surprised realizing Donna already knew who we were. She did not answer.

AFTER THE REUNION: A STORY OF ACCEPTANCE
Grace LaJoy Henderson

I felt embarrassed for my mother because I knew she had been living in denial about having children for forty-nine years. I knew she had not revealed to anyone that she had children. She seemed like she was pleased to have us there, but was not so proud of herself for having kept her very painful past a secret for so long.

After that very uncomfortable moment was over, my mother looked over at us and asked us how our morning had been. As I was telling her about our morning, I noticed her fingernails, freshly polished with a shiny reddish-orange polish. She asked if I had heard from Carla. I told her I had not and reminded her that my sister was still missing.

AFTER THE REUNION: A STORY OF ACCEPTANCE
Grace LaJoy Henderson

Chapter 7

DAY TWO OF OUR VISIT –
TALKING WITH MOTHER

"Do you know where Carla's husband is?" Mother inquired.

I told her Carla did not have a husband. She never married.

"Carla took the role as my parental figure for six years.

"After Daddy had left us in that house alone when I was seven, landing us in foster care, he regained full custody of us three years later. The first two years after he had gotten us back, he took us with him whenever he traveled. He was determined to never leave us again.

"Devotedly, he sat in the audience when Carla walked across the stage to get her high school diploma at age seventeen. He stood up and screamed, 'Go Carla!' That surprised me because he did not usually do things like that. He was so proud of her.

"He did his best to stay with us. That is, until Carla turned eighteen. Jerome, Grayson and Terrance were in the military. Daddy began traveling again, without us. This time, leaving Danisha and me to live with Carla, who was now a legal adult. I

59

lived with her from ages twelve through seventeen.

"She was kind of like a mother to me. I had to ask for her permission to go places. My big sister would say, 'You can go after you clean up that kitchen.'

"I would beg to wear her clothes and shoes.

"She would say, 'No, they are too big for you.'

"I would plead with her until, finally, she would say, 'Go ahead and wear them.'"

We all laughed.

Arica asked, "Oh, did you know that my mom was homecoming queen at her high school?"

My mother said, "Oh. You were?"

"Yes, I was Football Homecoming Queen," I said.

Mother laughed.

Then she remembered how when she was in grammar school, the boys and girls who sold the most cookies were crowned king and queen. She remembered that the homecoming ceremony was celebrated on May Day, of each year. She said her school had relay races first thing in the morning. "Then in the evening we had May Day," she recalled.

I asked her what grade she went to in school.

She said she went to the twelfth grade.

"But I was in a different place back then," she said.

"What place were you in?" Arica asked.

She told Arica the name of the city and state she was in back then. I was impressed with the way Arica asked her for clarification at a moment when I was wondering what "a different place" meant, but had not thought to ask.

I asked my mother if she went to college.

She said, "No. I just finished school, that's all."

I asked her how old she was when she first got married.

She said, "I was twenty. I had just got my first job."

I asked her what she did at her first job and she said she hung up coats and put them in place.

Then she continued her story, "So after I got my job, I worked there for two years. Then that's when I met my husband. There was a girl who worked at the same place where I worked. So, she asked me 'You want to come over my sister's house with me?' I said, 'Yeah, I'll go.' So, at her sister's house, that is where I met my husband."

She told me that she and my father moved to another state where he got a job, and they lived there for about eight years. One day he told her he had to go to Arizona for work.

She said, "So, he traveled around all over, you know, to get a job. Sometimes he would leave me there, sometimes about a week and sometimes about two weeks before he would come back."

Keeping my emotions bottled up was impossible. "Wow!" I exclaimed as the reality of that truth weighed on me.

I knew my father had left my five siblings and me in a house alone so that he could go work in Florida. But, I never knew that was something he often did before my mother left. When he left my siblings and me in that house alone, when I was seven, I thought it was the first time he had done such a thing.

Arica asked, "What was it about him that you decided to marry him?"

This question made us all laugh.

I think my mother was actually blushing as she explained, "Oh, he was nice and he was always helpful to me." She continued, "Yeah, he was nice to me and the kids, and like I said, he worked out of town, you know. And his boss would send him different places. When you're doing cement finishing, as soon as they would finish on one job, he'd go to another one. His boss would give him a job someplace else. Just on and on, we traveled around for a while. I liked the places he took me. Yeah uh huh."

Arica asked her which child she gave birth to first, Devon or Carla?

She said, "Devon," referring to my older brother Jerome, whom she called by his middle name.

"And after that you had Carla?" Arica asked.

"No, Grayson was number two. I wanted a girl. But, it didn't come as a girl. It came as a boy. I said, 'Another boy?'" she laughed. "So, then I had Carla."

I asked her if she was happy that she had her girl.

She said, "Yeah."

We all laughed.

She smiled, "I had my girl. She was as cute as a button."

Then mother looked at me and said, "You were the last one. Grace was the last one."

I asked her if she remembers having me.

She smiled and said, "Yeah."

Still talking about me, she continued, "She was a real fat baby. She was the cutest thing you ever want to see."

Then she said Terrance was born after Carla.

I asked, "And then Danisha?"

She said, "Yeah."

While talking about the birth order of the children she and my father had together, she tried to quote my birthplace, Terrance's birthplace, and Danisha's birthday. She quoted them all wrong. Then she said, "I had everything written down. But, after my stuff was stolen, it was misplaced, I had to write it all down again. Grace was the last one. She was bad, too!"

We all laughed.

I clarified, "You said she was bad?"

She said, "Yeah."

I joked, "That hasn't changed."

We all laughed.

Sometimes, it seemed like my mother did not realize she was actually talking to me when she recalled memories about "Grace." I found that intriguing. I asked her if she remembered walking me to a convenience store in Kansas City.

She said, "No."

Mother often answered with one word.

"Do you remember walking to the store and taking me with you? My brothers and sisters would be at school and Daddy would be at work. You would buy me chocolate covered malt balls and the clerk would hand them to me."

I laughed as I told her how, for years, I had been sharing the story of how the store clerk would *give* me malt balls. Later realizing that *she* had actually paid for the candy and the clerk was merely *handing* it to me.

"Malt balls are my favorite candy to this day because of that."

She said, "Oh yeah?"

I said, "Yeah."

Then I told her I remembered going into the closet, in her and my father's bedroom, trying to put on her clothes and shoes.

Mother did not seem to think that story was funny. In fact, she looked agitated when I was talking about putting on her clothes and shoes. Seeing the disturbed look on her face made me feel like this could be an example of why she said I was "bad." I do remember her picking me up taking me away from her closet and as soon as she was not looking, I went right back in.

To lighten the moment, Arica asked her which city was her favorite of all the cities she had been to. She said it was the outskirts of Los Angeles, California.

She explained, "We lived in a suburban area. And uh, it never got too cold and it never got too hot. It was pleasant all the time in that area. But, up in the mountains of Los Angeles, there was snow. We never had snow."

Arica asked her how she ended up in her current city and state.

"Oh, I had a friend that came here and he brought me along."

Then she digressed to talking about a job she had at a toy manufacturing company while she and my father were together. "I got a job so I could help bring some money in." She recalled how she was able to use her employee discount to buy toys for her children.

She remembered buying a toy oven for Carla.

"It had a little stove and a little sink and you put the water in the back in a container. Then you'd turn on the faucet and the water really came out of the faucet. And then it was an iron, you know, it didn't get hot, just warm enough where they wouldn't burn themselves. Carla loved that! She would say, 'Mommy, help me bake a cake.' So, it baked little cakes and cookies and they loved that."

We all smiled.

I told my mother that Carla had raved about that toy oven for years; and how she would always tell the story of how it was a gift from her mother, listing each and every function it would perform.

Arica asked my mother what is her favorite thing to do currently. I do not think she understood Arica's question.

She answered, "Well, I haven't been around them in a while. It's a long story. But, I'm trying to get things together where I can see my family again."

"We would love it if you came to Kansas City, but we also know that you have a home here and you are used to being here and you're probably comfortable here. It's like, it's kind of scary. I wouldn't want to move to another state. So, like why would you want to?"

"Right. It's a nice place to live for now. You never know

AFTER THE REUNION: A STORY OF ACCEPTANCE
Grace LaJoy Henderson

what's going to happen when you look ahead, you know. Right now, you know, I'd rather stay here, you know."

Those were her exact words.

Hearing her say this solidified my understanding of the fact that she would prefer to stay where she is for now. However, this was a great opportunity for me to pull out the assisted living information.

AFTER THE REUNION: A STORY OF ACCEPTANCE
Grace LaJoy Henderson

Chapter 8

DAY TWO OF OUR VISIT – TALK ABOUT MOVING

"Well, I *did* bring you some information, because Terrance and I would like for you to have it. I had intended on giving it to you yesterday, before you made it clear that you would really like to stay here. But when I told Terrance about it last night, he insisted I give you the information so you could have it. We realize it's your decision to make, but we at least want you to take a look, to know exactly what opportunities lie ahead in case you change your mind."

"Yeah. You never know what's up ahead," she agreed as I pulled out the folder.

I showed her the information for the one assisted living facility in Kansas City I had narrowed down for her. I told her it was just like where she currently lives except she would have her own room. I continued, "You would not have to live with anybody and you can leave your belongings in your room because it would be safe. You would not have to carry anything around for fear of it being stolen. It is a safe place, with twenty-four-hour security,

where you could come and go as you please just like you do here."
I told her that some of the benefits were weekly housekeeping,
laundry service, three meals a day, and medication management.
"The nurses come to your room to assist you with taking your
medication."

Mother seemed a little nervous when I mentioned the
medication part. I felt it was because of what Donna had told me
about the issues they had with her not taking her pills and hiding
them under her mattress.

"All utilities are included except phone. However, we
would provide a phone if you wanted one. This place would empty
your trash and provide transportation if you need to run errands.
They provide many activities and take the residents on outings,
like ball games. They even have a chapel for religious services,
and a beauty shop on the campus."

Mother asked, "They have a hairdresser right there?"

"Yes, and if you didn't have the money, *we* would pay for
it. We would make sure you had whatever you wanted.

"The room is not furnished so we would have to go and
pick out a nice bedroom set, with a comfortable mattress, and a
television. You would have a private bathroom with a walk-in
shower. The doctor, dentist, podiatrist, and psychiatrist are on site
regularly. You would be able to get treatment and rehabilitation
for your hip without having to leave the facility. They provide

behavioral health as well as assistance with bathing and grooming for those who need it."

Just then, a man walked out of the center room and through the lobby, where we were sitting. He looked over at us.

Mother jokingly said to him, "What are you being nosy over here for? What are you looking for?"

When the man was out of sight, I continued, "This particular place has a couple of rooms open at this time. However, if you decide to move a year or two down the road, we would have to check and see if they have a room available at that time."

Mother said, "Right."

I jokingly said to her, "If you wanted to go home with us now, then they would have a spot for you today."

We all laughed.

Every once in a while, as I was talking about the facility, Mother would say, "Right." This made me feel like she was listening with interest and that she was okay with me continuing to tell her more.

I felt like I had said enough, but I wished I had some pictures of the facility to show her. Arica found some pictures of it on her cell phone and showed them to her. As we looked at the pictures, Arica and I pointed out the beautiful dining area, the bedroom, and the private bathroom.

She said, "Wow! That's nice, real nice. Oh, boy! I haven't made up my mind yet."

"I want to go ahead and leave this information with you so you can take all the time you need to look at it and think about it.

She reiterated, "That looks like luxury! I'm not ready for anything like that yet. But, I'll give thought to it."

As we were finishing our assisted living discussion, I told her, "It would be nice if you lived in Kansas City because we are not always able to travel here to visit you."

I assured her, "If you were to move, you would still be in control of your own independence. We would not control your life. We would only be there for what *you* wanted us to be there for."

This portion of our visit ended with her saying, "I'll keep it in mind."

Then we moved on to talk about other things.

I told Mother that Terrance, Grayson, and Devon wanted to do a video call with her while Arica and I were there with her. I told her we had planned to do it Saturday if that was okay with her. She said it was okay and said four o'clock would be the best time for her.

I reminded her that Arica and I were taking her out to eat at one o'clock on Sunday. She had forgotten but she said she had wanted to go to Applebee's for a long time. After a revelation such as this it was no brainer where we would be dining on Sunday.

I asked her if there was anything she needed that we could bring to her while we were in town. She said, "Do you really want me to tell you? Money!"

We all laughed.

I told her we would give her some money before we left to go home. At that point, I realized that money was the best thing we could provide to her.

The Center Counselor, Rashad, came out into the lobby at around two o'clock and asked me if I would go into the hallway to chat with him. The center was to close at three o'clock, so he wanted to have time to chat with me before then.

I asked Mother if it was okay for him to talk to me.

She said, "Yes."

He and I entered the hallway. He expressed that he was very happy to know Geneva had family who cared about her. He had a puzzled look on his face as he revealed to me that Geneva had never mentioned having children. He conducts group sessions with the residents, and she would often shy away from group discussions about family.

I had already heard April and Donna say she never mentioned having children in the many years that they had been working with her. However, when he said it, I felt a sting in my emotions.

How could my mother have lived in denial about having children for so many years? This caused me to open up and begin to talk. Rashad showed great care and concern as he listened to my finding mother story.

As I recounted my side of events, he remained silent, observing me and nodding on occasion to let me know he was paying attention. I told him details about how she left, how I searched and how we recently reunited. I expressed how I had longed to find her and take care of her. I let him know that my ultimate purpose for being there was to woo her into moving closer to us so I could provide for her the way I had always wanted to.

He told me how amazing my story was and asked me a few questions, like, "So, is your father still alive?" and other similar questions. Then he began to tell me the true purpose of asking me to join him in the hallway.

He asked me if I would sign a release form so that he could be free to speak with me anytime concerning my mother's status at the center. I felt pressured even though I knew that was not his intention. He was just performing the part of his job that required him to obtain social history for Geneva, and to build a relationship with her family members. The pressure came from knowing I was not the average family member.

I explained that I was not sure if I wanted to take long-distance responsibility for her so soon after meeting her. I explained that it had been almost fifty years since I had seen her last and that I do not really know her. I felt afraid to commit to any responsibility I would have to take from so many miles away. I told him I had been talking with her about moving to Kansas City to be closer to us so, in which case I would be very comfortable taking full responsibility for her. However, it would be difficult to take care of her when we are in two different states.

I expressed that if she does not even want to be close to us, then why should I commit to taking any responsibility for her?

What he was asking me to do caused me to experience a lot of turmoil, stress and feelings of guilt the whole time we were talking. The thought of receiving a long-distance phone call, that my mother needed help, terrified me. I knew I would be limited to how much I could do because of the distance between us.

Would I sacrifice time and resources to go to her?

Probably not, because I felt like she left years ago because she did not want to be with us. Now she is refusing to live closer to us. So, why should I feel obligated at this stage of our lives?

Sure, I was enjoying her company during our visit, but that did not mean I wanted this type of responsibility for her, at least not long-distance. I told him I would take the form with me, share it with my brothers and give it some thought. He said that would be okay and gave me his card, which included his cell phone number. He invited me to call him anytime.

He confirmed that my mother had a mental illness and he told me her diagnosis. I am purposely not sharing the name of her diagnosis. However, the most common symptoms are delusions, hallucinations, disorganized thinking, abnormal behavior, and not able to function normally. Patients do not necessarily display all the symptoms all of the time. Symptoms range from remission to very severe.

As I considered what the counselor was telling me about my mother's mental illness, I was able to recall observing some of these symptoms in my mother.

During this moment with the counselor, I also thought back about the times when Ashley and Donna had told me about her occasional resistance to take her medication. I thought about how April and Donna told me that as long as she takes it, she is nice and does not bother anybody. However, if she refuses to take it, her uncontrollable behavior places her at risk of being committed, against her will, to a mental hospital.

The counselor went on to explain that one of the main goals of the center was to reunify residents with their family, if possible. He felt like it would be in her best interest to live near her children who loved her and wanted to take good care of her. He encouraged me to stay in touch with her, and said that he would do everything he could to encourage her to make an educated decision to come live with us in Kansas City. In the meantime, he would use group sessions to learn more about her desires and let me know her wants and needs so I could provide some things for her.

On the happy side, he told me she had an interest in knitting. On the unhappy side, he informed me she had been robbed and was afraid of it happening again. He revealed that was how her stuff, that she was telling Arica and I about, got "misplaced."

I paused to think about how a robber had taken her state identification, social security card, birth certificate, and all of her children's information.

This was very hurtful to hear.

I was distressed to know this horrific thing had happened to my own mother. I know it was impossible for me to have been able to protect her from that, but it did not stop me from wishing I could have.

We ended our conversation with him telling me to think about signing the release and to let him know what I decide to do. It was about fifteen minutes before the center would be closing when I returned to the lobby.

While I was in the hallway talking with the counselor, Arica and Mother had remained in the lobby and continued to talk. When I entered, Arica was asking her one question after another, her face flushed with anticipation of what each answer would be.

"How did you find out your adoptive mother was not your real mother?

"Did you ever want to meet your real mom?

"What can I call you, Grandmother, Nanny, Nana?

"What was it like when you first met my mom and her brothers? Were you surprised?

"What is your favorite childhood memory?"

I sat down and listened with much interest as Mother happily answered every one of Arica's questions. The smile and proud look on my mother's face let me know she was enjoying her talk with Arica.

In response to the questions, she said she was sixteen years old when she found out she was adopted, but she did not care because she was used to living with the woman who she called Mother. She said she had the opportunity to meet her biological mother. As far as what name Arica could call her, she said she would prefer for Arica to "just make it simple" and call her Geneva.

I felt a bit sad for my daughter because I believed she expected to be able to use some sort of endearment term to refer to her newly found grandmother. Arica later said she was okay with it and that she did not care.

"I don't really see her as my grandmother anyway," she said.

However, I still felt gloomy because I knew she was missing the experience of having a "normal" grandmother-granddaughter relationship with my mother.

I felt surprised, yet grateful when Arica asked the question about how Mother felt when she met us. That is something I would never have had the courage to ask. Mother admitted she was surprised and shocked when we showed up.

"I didn't know really what to say when they first came there. Because I don't usually have company. I never had real company, so I didn't know *what* to say!" she said.

I was very interested in what she had to say about meeting us for the first time.

Finally, she shared her favorite childhood memory.

She told Arica and me, "Mother and Father bought me a bike. I would see other kids riding their bikes on this hill and I wished I could ride a bike. So, I saw this bike in this yard. I said, 'I'm going to learn how to ride a bike.' So, I picked it up and went up the hill with the other kids. I went up and down, up and down, until I finally learned how to balance the bike. I was so happy I didn't know what to do! I was telling my girlfriend and some other kids, 'I learned how to ride a bike!'"

She continued, "My mother had told me to stay off bikes. She would say, 'You might fall and hurt yourself.' I *did* fall and the bike didn't even have brakes on it! I took a chance trying to learn, and skinned my knee. But, I said I don't care, I know how to ride a bike now!"

We all laughed.

She continued her story, "All of a sudden, I got afraid. I said, 'Oh my God!' My mother is gonna know that I was on the bike. My knee was skinned up. I said, 'I don't care, I know how to ride a bike!' So, when I got home, I was trying to hide it.

"Mother said, 'How did you get that scar?'

"I said, 'Oh, I just fell.'

"I didn't tell her about the bike.

"She put some peroxide on it to clean it. She felt sorry for me so she didn't spank me that time.

"So about two weeks after that, Mother and Father surprised me with a new bike!

"I said, 'That's all mine?'

"We had a large back yard. My mother wanted me to ride it in the back yard.

"I said, 'You don't ride bikes in the back yard.'

"I wanted to ride on the street. The other kids rode *theirs* on the street. Little by little, I eased up and started riding on the sidewalk. Then, little by little, I eased to the street. My mother put a bell and a basket on it. So, if I had to go to the store for her, she let me ride the bike."

When my mother finished telling us her new bike story, she explained that she had to ease from the backyard to the street when she got her first pair of skates, too. Before she got her own pair, she had found an abandoned pair on the sidewalk and put them on.

Her mother asked her where she got them.

She answered, "From the sidewalk. Nobody wants them or they wouldn't have left them out here."

Her mother made her put them back.

Soon after, she received her first pair of new skates.

Three o'clock came and our visit ended with all of us laughing about my mother's skate story.

As we were preparing to walk out, I felt proud of Arica for asking so many questions that I would not have thought to ask. I felt elated that my mother was feeling comfortable enough to provide responses.

We walked with mother as she carried her backpack to the elevator to get on the bus heading back to the boarding home. As mother was getting on the elevator, we told her we would be coming to visit her later that evening.

We went back to our hotel, ate a late lunch and got some rest. By then, it was time for us to go visit Mother. Nothing notable happened during that visit. We just sat in the living room, engaged in small talk and looked at the movie that was on the television. We also looked at some more pictures. After a nice and relaxing visit, Arica and I went out for dinner, returned to our hotel and retired to our rooms for the night.

As I lay my head on my pillow to rest for the night, I swirled in my mind what that day had brought about? I learned the true purpose of the center. That it was not merely a place for fun activities, but behavior therapy. We had the wonderful opportunity to talk to my mother, laugh with her, ask her many questions, and listen as she shared loving memories from her childhood. I got the chance to tell her all about the Kansas City assisted living facility I had in mind for her.

Most of all, one of my goals for the trip was fulfilled.

I finally found out how my mother truly felt about moving to Kansas City. I was finally able to stop worrying and relax, accepting that she is okay where she is for now. Like she said, "You never know what the future may hold."

Chapter 9

DAY THREE OF OUR VISIT - SATURDAY

I felt good on Friday, like half of my mission had been accomplished. However, there was still another goal to fulfill. I was not worried because I knew Mother and I would be talking Sunday, so Saturday was just a day to relax and enjoy our time together in the city, before going back to visit her. Arica and I sat outside in the city's downtown area and ate lunch that afternoon.

When we arrived at the boarding home that evening, Mother and the other residents were still sitting in the dining room area eating dinner. She did not see us walk in. We went into the dining room, walked over to two empty chairs at one of the tables and sat down. When she finally saw us, she looked a little puzzled to realize we had been sitting there without her being aware we were there. It was not clear to me exactly why she seemed puzzled.

After a couple of minutes, she asked us to go sit in the living room and wait for her. We sat in there and talked, while also glancing up at the television every once in a while. We waited for her for so long that we began to wonder where she was and what

AFTER THE REUNION: A STORY OF ACCEPTANCE
Grace LaJoy Henderson

she was doing. We knew she had probably long since finished eating her dinner. Before we arrived, I remembered that my brothers would be waiting for me to call them for a video call with Mother. The time came and she had not come into the living room yet, so I actually forgot about the video call.

After waiting for about fifteen more minutes, I was still wondering why mother was taking so long to join us. I left out of the living room to see where she was and what she was doing. One of the residents noticed I was looking for her and told me she was outside smoking. I went back and sat down on the couch until another fifteen minutes went by.

Finally, I made my way outside so I could see exactly what she was doing for myself. I found her sitting on the front steps of the boarding home, with her backpack sitting beside her, slowly savoring a cigarette. I figured that was her regular routine when we were not there. I presumed she needed that moment to herself before coming in to hang out with us.

When she saw me come outside, she told me she had given a young man some money and sent him to the store to buy Arica and me some bottles of soda pop. She said she would be in just as soon as he returned. I felt impressed that she thought of the idea to buy us something to drink. We were not big soda pop drinkers, but I did not tell Mother because I felt grateful that she thought of us in that way. I thought that was a very nice thing for her to do.

I went back into the house, strolled back into the living room and sat back down on the couch.

After a while, Mother finally entered the living room with a big smile on her face. Her backpack was in one hand, and two bottles of soda pop was in the other. She held the necks of the bottles in between her fingers. The proud look on her face indicated that she was confident we would be happy about getting the drinks; and that we would feel it was worth the wait to quench our thirst at last.

She gave us our drinks, set her backpack down and sat in between us on the couch.

Suddenly I remembered the video call!

First, I made a video call to Terrance and Grayson. They had agreed to wait together over Grayson's house, since Terrance's phone did not have video call option. When they did not answer the call, I tried several more times. By this time, I was feeling very disappointed with myself for forgetting, and I was feeling bad for having kept them waiting.

They never did answer, so I called Jerome, who answered immediately. He and his wife came face-to-face with Mother and enjoyed a wonderful video call.

After that, I made a regular voice call to Terrance and found out he had already left Grayson's house. They had waited for my call for an hour, then gave up. I told him how sorry I was and that if he went back around to Grayson's house, I would call again. He assured me it was okay and said he did not have time to go back over.

I take pride in being a person who keeps my word.

Knowing my brothers were waiting and I did not call, made me feel awful. I got over it for the moment, and showed Mother some more of the family photos I had brought. We looked at photos, while glancing up at the television every now and then.

I looked over and noticed Arica had not opened her soda pop. I realized she was not going to drink it because she does not drink pop. I am the same, but I drank it for two reasons: I actually like the flavor that she bought and could not resist, and I truly appreciated her kind gesture.

While my mother was engrossed with turning pages in my picture album, I looked at her and noticed some similarities. I had always wondered why my legs, toes and forehead looked the way they do. They look similar to hers, except her features were more pronounced than mine.

All of a sudden, I heard someone shout, "Medication!" It was a worker in the office. This was a call for all residents to come over to the office door, stand in line and take their medication. Mother continued to look at photos until Arica and I asked her if she needed to take her medication.

She said she would take it later.

Just then, I remembered the story Donna told me about my mother hiding medication under her mattress and not taking it.

I said, "You better go take your medication."
She looked at me with an understanding look on her face, got up off the couch, walked over to the office door, stood in line and took her pill. As she was walking back towards us, I noticed she walked on her tiptoes and did not pick her feet up all the way when she walked. It reminded me of the way my father would often scold me. He would say, "Stop walking on your tip toes!" and "Pick your feet up when you walk!"

I also noticed my sense of humor was similar to hers. She understood all of my jokes and I understood hers. We laughed at each other's witticisms. Realizing where I got some of my features and characteristics from caused me to appreciate myself more.

It was getting late and we needed to be getting back to the hotel. As we were wrapping up our visit, and putting away pictures, I reminded Mother we would be taking her out to dinner the next day.

She mentioned that she would be embarrassed about "hopping" into the restaurant due to her hip pain. However, she said she would go and told us to pick her up at one o'clock on Sunday. Hearing her comment about "hopping" into the restaurant made me think she was feeling hesitant about going out to eat with us. However, since she said she would go, I did not push the issue.

I hoped she would keep her promise to go with us. If I managed to take her out, it would be a thing to remember, not to mention that I truly needed to have *that* talk with her about why she left our family.

Arica and I said our goodbyes to Mother, then, we went to a restaurant to have dinner before going back to our hotel. Back at the hotel, I called Terrance again just to make sure he was not upset with me for forgetting to make the video call. Again, he told me it was okay. I offered to put them on a video call when we went back the next day. He told me not to worry about it and that he was fine with not having the call. From that conversation, I felt assured that he did not have any ill feelings about the situation.

I went to bed that night eagerly anticipating the next day, when I would finally have the talk with my mother that I had been waiting for.

Chapter 10

DAY FOUR OF OUR VISIT - SUNDAY

On Sunday morning, I woke up feeling very excited as I looked forward to taking my mother out to dinner and hearing her side of the story of why she left us forty-nine years ago. She had already promised we could discuss it. So, I was bursting with joy over what this day would bring. I was planning on striking up the conversation when we took her out for dinner. There we would have privacy away from the boarding home, in which people were always around.

For months, ever since our reunion visit, I had been looking forward to my mother talking to me about why she left.

I was not able to ask about it during the initial reunion visit because I felt like it was too soon since we had just met her again after so many years. It had taken a long time for her to finally open up to us during that visit. When she did, she only talked about positive things that made her smile. I sensed strongly that she would not feel comfortable opening up about why she left. So, I refrained from asking her about it at that time.

However, after my brothers and I had returned home from our initial reunion visit, I was talking to her on the phone. I had asked her if she would be okay with talking to me about why she left. She told me she would be okay with it, but she could not talk about it over the phone because office workers were listening and she did not want them to know her business. I was happy to learn that she was willing to talk about it. So, for months, I had looked forward to the precise moment in time that I would be sitting next to her listening as she openly shared her story.

After rising out of bed, Arica and I packed our suitcases, put them in the car and checked out of the hotel. We skipped breakfast in our anticipation of taking mother out to eat. Since she was expecting us to come at one o'clock, we had the entire morning to do whatever we wanted to do.

We went shopping.

I had observed that the flip-flop shoes she was wearing did not provide the support I felt she needed for her feet. So, I bought her some comfortable sandals and some socks before going over.

It was around noon when we finished shopping.

Having nothing else to do, we went on over to the boarding home. When we got there, we exited our vehicle and walked to the front of the boarding home. Geneva was sitting outside on the front steps smoking a cigarette.

"You all are early," she said.

AFTER THE REUNION: A STORY OF ACCEPTANCE
Grace LaJoy Henderson

I couldn't help but marvel at the way she was cognizant about the time of day. I had been carrying an incorrect assumption that she was not supposed to know what month, day or time it was due to her mental illness. As always, she was acutely aware.

We explained that we did not have anything else to do after shopping, so we just came on over.

Just then, she announced, "I'm not going!"

My excitement evaporated immediately at her words. That was a moment I had looked forward to for months. The moment that I would finally be able to spend time with her away from the boarding home and get the answers I needed about why she left our family.

In an instant, I remembered the evening before, when she talked about her reluctance to go out to eat with us. I recalled in my mind how she had mentioned feeling embarrassed about the idea of "hopping" into a restaurant due to her painful hip.

Even though I felt disappointed about her backing out, I understood where she was coming from. I could not be angry with her for deciding not to go. She had given us fair warning that she may be uncomfortable about going out in public. I just did not take full heed to her warning due to being so enthusiastic about the possibility of it all.

It quickly dawned on me that she was accustomed to being either at the boarding home or at the center. She had not been acclimated into going out to public places. So, although she said yes at first, I believe she changed her mind when she realized it would not be realistic for her to "limp" herself into a public place after being sheltered in mental health facilities for so many years.

After getting over the initial shock of her proclamation that she was not going, I noticed a lady sitting on the front steps smoking with my mother. She was a resident of the boarding home.

She introduced herself and asked who we were.

Geneva offered her usual answer of how it was none of her business who we were.

At the same time, I was saying, "This is *my* daughter," pointing at Arica, and "I am *her* daughter!" pointing at Geneva.

The woman said, "Geneva, I didn't know you had children!"

Geneva just stared ahead with a blank look on her face and did not respond. She did not seem upset about me telling her secret, however.

I realized she had lived in denial about having children for so many years and that she did not like people knowing her business. However, I got the feeling that she was okay with me telling the truth and that she would not dare want to risk crushing me by denying me to the woman after I had claimed her with so much excitement.

I wondered if she had been in denial as a way of burying the emotional pain and embarrassment of having left us so many years ago. Everyone who I met at the boarding home acted shocked about Geneva having children. Some of them had known her for over fifteen years, and they never had a clue she had given birth.

After a few moments, I accepted the fact that my mother was not going to allow us to take her out to eat.

In my heart, I still needed to hear her tell me her story of why she left.

I felt determined not to leave town without having that conversation with her. I offered to spend some time with her there at the boarding home before we got on the road back to Kansas City. She accepted my offer and seemed happy about having us stay and visit with her for a while. I told her I bought her some sandals and socks and that I was going to give them to her when we went out to eat. Since we were not going, I asked her if I could go get the items out of the car and give them to her.

She said that would be okay.

I went to the car and came back to the front of the house with the shopping bag in my hand. I took out the items and showed them to her. She tried on the shoes and said they were very comfortable. She really liked them a lot.

After she had finished smoking, she stood up and picked up her backpack. Then she invited us inside and asked, "Do you want to sit where we were sitting yesterday?" She was referring to the living room, where other residents were sitting and the television was up very loud, making it hard to hear each other talk.

This was my absolute last opportunity to talk to her about why she left and I knew it would be difficult, if not impossible to talk about it in the living room.

So, I responded, "No."

She said it was more comfortable in there.

I said, "It is? Oh okay."

We all went into the living room. Arica and I sat down on the couch. My mother announced she would be right back and left out of the room, leaving her backpack on the floor in front of the couch.

While she was gone, I expressed to Arica that I wished the television was not on. I was afraid it would interfere with my mission of talking with my mother about why she left. Not only was the television on, but once again it was very loud. I thought even if we were able to talk, we might not be able to hear each other.

We could not just turn it down because for one, it was mounted high up on the wall, not to mention that other people were watching it, *and* we were just the visitors with no say on the matter.

We chatted until finally my mother walked back in. She was wearing the comfortable sandals I had just given her.

I asked, "How do those feel?"

"Nice and comfy," she said, just before sitting down in between Arica and me on the couch. I did not bring any pictures for her to look at this time.

Mother asked us where we stayed, and we told her the name of the hotel. She had never heard of that hotel. She began to tell us about various other hotels that she knew about in the area.

As she was talking, I remembered how well Arica was able to inspire her to open up and talk on Friday. So, I asked Arica if she had any "questions." We both laughed because she knew exactly what I meant: the type of questions that would help my mother open up and give me the answers I so desperately needed from her. We were at the end of our visit and I wanted to hear her tell me her story of why she left. Arica did not have any questions at that time, but Mother did.

"Did you hear from Terrance?" she asked.

She was referring to the situation the day before when I failed to call Terrance and Grayson on time for the four o'clock video call as I had promised. I told her I had talked to him and he had forgiven me.

AFTER THE REUNION: A STORY OF ACCEPTANCE
Grace LaJoy Henderson

Chapter 11

DAY FOUR OF OUR VISIT – WHY MOTHER LEFT

Suddenly, mother started laughing about something on television. Feeling tensed, I was nervously trying to find a way to ask my mother about why she left.

Feeling afraid of her rejecting my inquiry, I began by saying, "So, you'll never tell me? I really want to know. You don't think you'll ever share?"

Somehow, she understood exactly what I was trying to say.

She responded, "I'm a private person."

Desperately trying to appease her with hopes she would open up and begin to give me the answers I needed, I replied, "I'm the same way. In fact, a lot of your children are the same way."

"Are they?" she said.

Still feeling extremely petrified I rambled, "So, I totally understand that. Yeah. But, I mean like I just really want to hear from you. You know. Because I've heard a lot of stuff. But, I just want to hear from you."

She said, "Right."

I continued, "I feel like I know. I just want to hear you say the actual words."

Mother had a nervous look on her face as she pointed at the woman who was working in the office.

"Can she hear us?" I asked.

She replied, "When we be on the phone, she eavesdrops and then she will gossip. So, I don't want to come right out with anything. You know?"

By now, I was feeling extremely discouraged.

I responded timidly, "Oh okay. That's why I thought we could talk since I'm here, and I don't know when I'll be back again. The next time I talk to you, it will probably be on the phone, and I *know* you will not be able to talk then. While I'm here, like this is like the perfect time. And if you can't talk now, then I guess, it's kind of like a now or never situation."

Mother laughed, "Now or never."

Unsure of what was funny, I told her, "That is how I feel."

She said, "That's the name of a song."

I responded, "Yep. Maybe we can go outside and talk."

Mother totally disregarded my request to go outside.

Looking up at the television, she asked, "That's the movie we saw last night, isn't it?"

"Yes, that's the same one," I said.

By that time, it appeared I would be going back to Kansas City without my concerns being satisfied. I knew once we left, I would never ever get the answers I needed so badly. I was feeling sad and disheartened, yet frustrated. The thought of leaving without hearing her story devastated me.

One of my two desires for returning had been met, but it seemed I would carry the other one for the rest of my life. As I basked in my feelings of desolation, my mother made a humorous comment about a commercial that came on television.

Feeling hugely embarrassed about what was happening, I looked over at Arica, who had been quiet the whole time, and saw her eyes were teary.

Finally, she said something.

"Miss Geneva," she said. "I know I don't know when we are going to see you again. I respect your decision not to share. I want you to know that there are a lot of us that have questions about our past. You know? Who we are, where we came from…"

"Right," said Mother.

Arica continued, "…Why we are the way we are. I know that some of the things my mom has been told has been hurtful to her. She's been told that you didn't want her. But, we don't know. You know it's like we just have questions…"

"Yeah," Mother agreed.

Arica continued, "If there was anything that you *did* feel comfortable sharing, could you share *something* that you do feel comfortable with? Just *anything* that is true so that we can fill in some holes, fill in some gaps…"

It was obvious to me that Arica's plea genuinely touched my mother's emotions and caused her to understand how important it was for her to open up and share her story.

It was at that point that I think my mother realized we had no intentions of leaving without the answers I needed.

Seeing the change in my mother's countenance caused me to feel so very grateful that Arica was there with me. She knew exactly the right words to say and how to articulate them in a way that pricked my mother's heart.

"Right. Well uh," Mother said.

Seeing she was ready to speak freely, I said, "We can go somewhere where it is quiet if you want."

Mother reverted, "Are you sure my husband is dead?" She was referring to my father.

I was feeling like, even though my mother was prepared to share, she was afraid to begin for fear my father could be still alive, for fear he would be upset with her for telling me her side of the story.

In response to her concern I said, "Yes. I am sure he has passed away." I stopped for a moment, trying to contain my emotions. "He and grandmother told me you left and you did not want me. But, even if that was the case, I forgive you."

Mother laughed a grateful laugh, as if she was relieved to hear me say that.

I continued, "But, I just want to hear the story from you, that's all."

Mother took a deep breath as if she tried to brace herself for what she was about to reveal.

"It all began before you were born. I would often feel tired from taking care of the five kids your father and I had together. He would go out of town for work, leaving me alone with them for one or two weeks at a time. I told him I needed a break from the kids..."

Clearly, it was hard for her to delve into her emotions and relive all of those unpleasant memories, but she was doing it for me.

From her story, coupled with things I already knew, I gathered that she had already been in and out of mental facilities several times before I was even born. I had concluded that she was a patient in a mental hospital at the time of my birth, and that my father had taken me home from the hospital. If he had not, the State of Michigan would have taken custody of me and would have likely gotten adopted – just like the additional four children she had after she left us. Somehow, between her hospital stays, our family ended up in Kansas City, where she experienced her final mental hospital stay before leaving our family for good.

Her story was somewhat choppy, so I had to piece things together. Nevertheless, I felt happy and relieved that she was finally opening up.

This was the moment I had been waiting to have with my mother.

I was basking in it as I listened intently to every word she had to say, even if the story was rather difficult to follow.

She continued, "My husband and my mother arranged to have me put in a hospital. They told me it was a regular hospital, that would help my body rejuvenate and give me some rest from the kids. After I was admitted, I found out it was a mental hospital. Your father thought it was just a normal hospital. He didn't know it was a mental hospital, you know."

Hearing her say this, I felt reasonably sure he knew but he and my grandmother just had to trick her into going because she may not have cooperated otherwise. I also felt reasonably sure that she was likely suffering from the symptoms of her mental illness during that time, and that was why they tricked her in that manner.

She went on, "I had a good up-bringing and a good relationship with my mother and my husband. They didn't really talk to me about personal stuff. They kept it to themselves. I really didn't know much, either, around that time. He didn't talk to me that much.

"He was nice to me. He just wanted me to feel better."

She recalled being in the mental hospital and no one ever coming to see her.

"He stayed away. My mother came only one time and she brought Danisha with her, and that was it. I was in that place for two years with no visitors."

Hearing that part of her story, I tried to put two-and-two together.

I thought, "She is saying she was in a mental facility for two years, with no visitors, just before she left. However, I was two years old when she left, and I have several specific memories of her being at home during the two years that she was claiming to have been locked away with no visitors."

I told her, "I specifically remember you being at home."

"I would come home on furlough." She said.

Hearing this part of her story brought back a vague memory that I had been carrying. I was a toddler, and my grandmother had driven me to the hospital where my mother was a patient. Anxious to see her, I was heartbroken when we arrived and I was not allowed to go into the area where her room was. Memories of why were not clear, but my devastation was vivid.

I realized that Mother was doing her very best to share only the things she was comfortable sharing. I also realized she could possibly be confused about the order in which some of the events took place so long ago.

I tried to refrain from thinking she would be purposely lying to me. Even if she was, I would still be understanding towards her because she has every reason to experience feelings of shame about the details of her past life.

She alleged, "There is a lot I don't know. I did not have a chance to talk to my husband before I left the mental hospital with my friend. He said he had family in another town so that is where we went."

As she was telling me that part of her story, I was thinking about how my father and grandmother told me she had professed, "I'm in love with Calvin," just before she ran away from the mental hospital.

"Did you at least say goodbye to Grandmother before you left?" I asked.

"Yes, I told her bye-bye."

She said a few more things, then, ended that part of her story by saying, "And that's all I know."

Although some of her story did not add up or match what I had always believed, I was still very appreciative that she had shared it with me. I told her I understood everything she had just expressed.

I mentioned that I remember my father hitting her a lot.

"Do you remember that?" I asked her.

"One time, we were on our way to church. Your father hit *at* me. He was angry about something, but never explained it to me. He just hit me, you know? And that's all it was."

I told her, "I remember him hitting you, and it was not right. I don't care what your mental state was, you did not deserve to be hit, ever."

She started talking about the people upstairs on the "third floor" again.

From my time with my mother, she usually starts reverting to the "third floor" to avoid dealing with the reality of painful memories. I believe the "people upstairs" were actually voices she was hearing in her head. However, she did not perceive the voices as being in her head. She believed they were in the same house with her, but on a different floor in the boarding home.

I was hoping she still had more to tell me about her story.

On the other hand, I was hoping she was feeling at peace about having opened up about things she had been keeping to herself for so many years.

I assured her, "You can tell me anything. There is not anything you could that would surprise me.

"I feel like I pretty much know the details surrounding why you left, but I just need to hear it from you."

Again, she reverted to talking about the voices from "upstairs." As an attempt to bring her focus back to our talk, I asked her some questions.

"Do you remember telling my father you were in love with Calvin?"

She said, "No, the people upstairs told him that."

"Do you remember saying you did not want your kids?"

"No, I never said anything like that. I was away from them for a long time. One time, I was in a mental hospital and the staff told me, 'Your family is here.'"

Mother's face displayed a look of distress.

"But, they never told me where you all were, and so I never knew what had happened to my family."

She looked down in sadness.

I was unable to place the exact timeframe of that incident, as she seemed confused about exactly when it had happened.

"Do you ever feel angry with my father for hitting you?"

"Besides the tap on my hand on our way to church, he treated me good. There is nothing for me to be angry about. He was nice to me otherwise, but it could have been something that was going on away from me and he didn't want to tell."

She continued, "We were on our way to church and he just, you know, he just spanked me on my hand like *that*."

She tapped me on my hand to show me how he had hit her.

Her recollection of my father's abuse was very surprising to me because I specifically remember my daddy beating on her. Furthermore, he never denied it. He specifically said he "had to knock some sense into her." It seemed to me she was in denial, and was making light of, and excuses for, my father's actions.

I told her, "I remember standing outside of your and his bedroom and hearing you crying as he was striking you. I would feel heartbroken. You did not deserve that."

She said, "He was nice to me, you know? I taught my children to love their father and they did."

I had spent many years thinking she had left because my father beat her. But, her responses to my questions made me feel like that was not the reason at all. In her mind, he was good to her and she had no reason to be angry with him. This left me with a new question:

"So, do you remember what caused you to leave?" I asked.

She answered in these exact words, "Let's see how did this start? It's been a long time. Oh yeah, we went to...after I was in the hospital for a while, they um sent me on a plane to go to Kansas City where my mother was. And so, after we stayed there for a while, he had a place... a house there and uh, so let's see...all the kids they were happy to see me and we were happy together, you know? Really, they loved me and I loved them. So, um, I was pregnant with you. And so, uh I had to go to the hospital and have you. And um…"

I interjected, "I had ordered my birth records and it looked like my daddy took me home from the hospital. It appeared you did not take me home."

She said, "Right. And I was in the hospital, too. They never talked to me about anything."

"Were you in a mental hospital at the time of my birth?"
She said, "Yes."

I told her, "I thought maybe that was the case, and maybe that was why you were not able to take me home."

She mentioned the people "upstairs" again. Then she mumbled something about my father still having their marriage license. It seemed like she was saying she was not sure if she and my father were divorced.

"Do you think you and my father are still married?"
She said, "Yes."

"After you left, the court granted him a divorce without you since you were not there anymore."

Most of the questions I asked her were based on negative memories and experiences, and I expected her to tell me she left because she was being beaten or that she was hurting, or perhaps because she was angry with my father or my grandmother.

But, none of those were the case.

She told me, "I didn't really know too much about the negative side because I was not around to know about it. All I knew was the positive side of the life I had with my family."

She admitted she left with Calvin because my father never came when she was in the mental hospital.

"Did you and Calvin get married?"

She said, "Yes," and told me the state where they were married, which explained why I was never able to find a marriage license for the two of them in the states where I was searching. I had no clue that Mother had ever been in the state where they actually got married. So, I had never searched there.

By now, it was clear that I had finally fulfilled my mission of hearing my mother tell me her story of why she left.

For so long, I felt like my mother had abandoned her family. However, after listening to her side of the story, it seems her family may have abandoned her long before she ever left. I have been feeling rejected for all of those years and it seems she may have, in a sense, been feeling rejected, too.

AFTER THE REUNION: A STORY OF ACCEPTANCE
Grace LaJoy Henderson

Chapter 12

DAY FOUR OF OUR VISIT –

RETURNING HOME

Arica sat patiently the whole time my mother and I were talking. Then she asked, "Are you doing okay?"

Mother said, "Yes, I'm okay."

With the stress of our conversation being over, Mother invited us to move from the living room into the dining room. As we were getting ready to leave the room, Arica offered to carry the backpack for her and she let her. Arica struggled greatly as she was picking it up. Then she looked at my mother as if to wonder how in the world this tiny, delicate looking woman has the strength to carry around such a heavy bag.

"Miss. Geneva, this is heavy! How do you do it?"

My mother replied, "I'm a strong woman, you just don't know!"

We all laughed.

During our entire visit, I had wondered what exactly was in that backpack.

After we had settled in the dining room, Arica thanked my mother for sharing her story.

She said, "You only shared what you were comfortable with right?"

Mother said, "Yes."

Then Arica asked some questions like, "Did you play the piano?" And, "Did you sing, too?"

Mother answered yes to both. Then she began to talk some more about people in the boarding home stealing her clothes and other belongings. "They even stole my Bible! Can you imagine who would want to steal a Bible? They don't read it!"

We all laughed.

I reminded her that is why I really wished she could move away from there and live closer to us. "I could take you shopping right now, but I know if you bring new things back here, someone would steal it. If you were there with us, you would have your own room, and we could buy you things without having to worry about it getting stolen."

She said, "That sounds good!"

I asked her if she was going be thinking about moving or if she pretty much knows she wants to stay there.

She admitted she likes where she is and that the stealing was not a factor in her decision to stay there. She reiterated that she likes that they have done many things to fix up the boarding home, like painting the walls. She said she likes the convenience of being close to the store, laundry mat, and bus stop.

I told her I understood. While I wish she felt differently, I accepted her reasons for wanting to stay where she was.

She said she was not sure how she had lost all of her children, that details of it were a blur and no one ever explained it to her. She recalled a time when she went back to a house, where children from her second marriage were living, and found the house boarded up.

"I felt devastated. I didn't know what had happened to my kids, or why they had taken them away."

My heart wept for her at that moment.

I told her I had taken some steps to search for them and asked if she knew the names of the hospitals where they were born. She gave me the names of the hospitals. I could not wait to get home and submit this information to Elsie to see if it would help her locate them in her database.

Our visit was rapidly ending. We used my cell phone to take some pictures with Mother. When I showed her one of the pictures on my cell phone screen, she said, "Wow, I am much prettier than I thought I was!"

We all smiled.

I kept my promise to give her some cash. To show me how much she appreciated the money, she smiled very big, told me "thank you" and gave me a great big kiss on my jaw. We gave our final goodbyes and hugs, then Arica and I walked out of the boarding home, went to the car, hopped in and headed towards the highway to begin our very long drive back to Kansas City.

Arica and I had enjoyed the city. We had partaken in great conversations with my mother, and I knew I had received all the answers I was to going to acquire from her. As we traveled home, I did a lot of thinking about how I felt our visit had gone. I appreciated my mother for doing the best she could to talk to me about why she left.

Even though she was forced to admit herself into a mental hospital around that time, and even though she said there was a lot that she, herself, still did not know surrounding that era, I still felt like there was more she could have shared with me.

I believed she was in denial about a lot of the ways she was feeling back then. I believed she may have been experiencing a lot of guilt for not wanting her children. She did not admit to not wanting us, but I believe it was true.

I valued the things she felt comfortable sharing, but I felt doubtful that she had truly given me all the facts. Therefore, I just had to accept the reality that I may never know her full story.

I wanted her to say she was ready to move, but she did not. The good thing is that I realized my mother's basic needs were being met. I was intrigued to learn that the center is not merely social engagement just to give boarding home residents something fun to do. It is actually a mental health treatment center.

Since she was satisfied to stay where she was, I had to accept the fact that she may never live in Kansas City with us.

Overall, I was impressed with the work of the boarding home and mental health treatment center. I realized they are committed to that specific community of people. They have taken on the challenge of providing their basic physical, emotional and mental health needs. I realized that if it were not for the boarding home and the center, every single person living there would probably be homeless. So, I appreciate the work they are doing and I am grateful they have provided a home for my mother.

Even though I knew exactly how my mother felt about staying where she was for now, I still had a strong desire for her to move closer to us. I did not want any mother of mine to have to carry a heavy backpack around all the time. I imagined her being able to leave her belongings in a room of her own, that she does not have to share. I imagined her having a key to her own room and not having to worry about the other residents coming in and taking her stuff. It was hard for me to wipe out the images in my head of her carrying that big black backpack everywhere she went.

Ultimately, I felt like I got the answers I traveled so many miles for.

I felt grateful that Arica was there with me. I never would have gotten the answers I needed without her. When I took her with me, I did not think about the fact that I was actually taking a licensed social worker with me. I just figured I was taking my daughter for companionship and support. However, having her with me made a world of difference and I cannot begin to imagine how the trip would have gone without her being there.

Due to some things being a blur, Mother was not able to provide clear answers for all of my questions surrounding her departure. However, she gave her sincere responses to my two inquiries. So, I felt like I could not ask for anything more than that.

Nevertheless, a part of me still felt a little disheartened that my two desires remained only partially fulfilled. Therefore, the end of this trip served as time of overall acceptance:

Accepting that Mother actually did not want me, that she left me in the hospital when I was born, and that she left four additional children after she left our family of six children.

Accepting that she left of her own accord, not because of anything my father or grandmother had done.

Accepting that she is mentally ill; that this nice, smart woman is actually sick, and unable to be a mother to me.

Accepting the horrific fact that someone robbed her.

Accepting her poverty-stricken living environment; that

she is happy where she is; and that she is not interested in allowing us to provide a better life for her in Kansas City.

Accepting the fact that I may never get her full story without her referring to the people on the "third floor."

I felt I had no choice but to accept all of these things, since this is the way things are and I cannot change it. This left me with a lot of thoughts and feeling as Arica and I were leaving, returning home to Kansas City.

For the next few months after that visit, I experienced an assortment of emotions. I am very transparent about them in the next book from the *Finding Mother Series* entitled, *Diary of Emotions: Thoughts and Feelings.*

Discussion Questions

1. Name at least three (3) common symptoms of Mother's diagnosis.

2. Did Mother exhibit any of these symptoms? If so, which ones?

3. Discuss the difference between an assisted living facility and a nursing home.

4. What are your thoughts about the author's phone conversations with Mother.

5. The author thought Mother's center was a place that merely provided fun activities. What was it instead? What, if any, thoughts do you have about that?

6. Why do you think the center manager allowed Geneva to skip the center activities and talk with the author and Arica instead?

7. Mother never wanted more than two children. She ended up having ten and left them all. Do you think Mother would have still run away if she had only had the two children she desired? Why or why not? Discuss your response.

8. Mother told Arica how she felt when the author and her brothers first showed up to reunite with her. What are your thoughts about how Mother felt?

9. Discuss why you think mother changed her mind about going out to eat with the author?

10. Name three (3) ways the author showed "Acceptance."

Questions Teachers Can Ask

*Critical Thinking/In-depth Comprehension/Writing
Skills/Technology Skills*

1. What is the main idea or learning experience of the book?

2. Write your thoughts or feelings about the story or your favorite character.

3. Summarize your favorite part of the book and tell why this was your favorite part.

4. Write about an experience in your personal life and tell how it is similar to this story.

5. Write a summary of the story, highlighting what you think the main issues are.

6. To whom would you recommend this book? Why?

7. How can the information in the story be useful in your life or future?

8. Research a famous or infamous person on the computer who has had a similar experience, and write a report about that person's life.

Further Discussion Points

After the Reunion indicated some of Geneva's Symptoms, Coping Behaviors, and Treatments for her mental illness. It also indicated some Effects this has had on the author. Below are some excerpts, from the book, that you may use for additional discussion.

Symptoms

Hallucinations. One symptom of Geneva's diagnosis is hallucinations. She often referred to the things she was hearing from "people upstairs on the third floor." Geneva seemed to be having *auditory* hallucinations. Read and discuss the excerpts below.

However, whenever the subject came up of why she left our family, she would either start talking about something else, or tell me about the things she was hearing from the "people on the third floor." **Page 11** Note: this could also be avoidance.

I believe the "people upstairs" were actually voices she was hearing in her head. However, she did not perceive the voices as being in her head. She believed they were in the same house with her, but on a different floor in the boarding home. **Page 105**

She said, "No, the people upstairs told him that." **Page 106**

Accepting the fact that I may never get her full story without her referring to the people on the "third floor." **Page 117**
Note: this could also be avoidance.

Coping Behaviors

Denial. When the author and her siblings went to reunite with Geneva, she denied them at first, then later accepted them. Read and discuss the excerpt below.

AFTER THE REUNION: A STORY OF ACCEPTANCE
Grace LaJoy Henderson

During our reunion visit, I noted that the more she looked at the pictures, the more it began to "click" for her that we were her children. The more she realized we were her children, the more she opened up, and eventually accepted us. To say that the pictures were a powerful tool would be an understatement. **Page 35**

Denial. Geneva had been in denial about having children for all of the years the she has been gone. The boarding home workers, center manager, her counselor, NOBODY knew she had children when the author and her siblings went to reunite and visit with her. Therefore, she had kept this secret to herself for almost 50 years! Read and discuss the excerpts below.

I told her I was Geneva's daughter and that my siblings and I had found her after forty-nine years. She expressed a variety of feelings. "Oh my, I am so excited that the two of you are here! This is a surprise! I never even knew Geneva had children! **Page 54**

I felt embarrassed for my mother because I knew she had been living in denial about having children for forty-nine years. I knew she had not revealed to anyone that she had children. **Page 57**

The woman said, "Geneva, I didn't know you had children!" Geneva just stared ahead with a blank look on her face and did not respond. **Page 92**

I wondered if she had been in denial as a way of burying the emotional pain and embarrassment of having left us so many years ago. **Page 93**

Everyone who I met at the boarding home acted shocked about Geneva having children. Some of them had known her for over fifteen years, and they never had a clue she had given birth. **Page 93**

Guilt. The author believed that Geneva was feeling guilty for abandoning them. Read and discuss the excerpt below.

I believed she may have been experiencing a lot of guilt for not wanting her children. **Page 114**

Avoidance. Geneva said, on several occasions, that she had "business" to take care of before she could reunite, move closer, move forward with her relationship with the author and her siblings. Read and discuss the excerpts below.

When I asked her if I could help her take care of her business, she said she could do it herself. **Page 11**

Eventually, I began to wonder if she really had "business," or if she was just trying to protect my feelings because she did not know how to tell me that moving closer to us, and allowing us to take care of her, was never in her plans. **Page 11**

Avoidance. Whenever the author tried to talk about something Geneva was not comfortable talking about, Geneva would start talking about the people "upstairs" on the "third floor" even though there was no third floor in the boarding home. Read and discuss the excerpts below.

She started talking about the people upstairs on the "third floor" again. From my time with my mother, she usually starts reverting to the "third floor" to avoid dealing with the reality of painful memories. **Page 105**

"I feel like I pretty much know the details surrounding why you left, but I just need to hear it from you." Again, she reverted to talking about the voices from "upstairs." **Page 106**

"Were you in a mental hospital at the time of my birth?" She said, "Yes." I told her, "I thought maybe that was the case, and maybe that was why you were not able to take me home." She mentioned the people "upstairs" again. **Page 108**

Treatments. Treatment for Geneva has included:

- **Medication**
- **Psychosocial Intervention**
- **Hospitalization**

Medication. The mental illness that Geneva has affects her actions, thoughts and feelings. It causes her to see the world differently from someone who does not have a mental illness. This means she may try to avoid taking her medication. Sometimes it may be challenging to get her to cooperate. Read and discuss the excerpts below.

The staff came up with a bright idea to check under the mattress on her bed. There they found the pills she was supposed to be taking daily, but she had been hiding them instead. **Page 55**

I told her that some of the benefits were weekly housekeeping, laundry service, three meals a day, and medication management. "The nurses come to your room to assist you with taking your medication." Mother seemed a little nervous when I mentioned the medication part. **Page 70**

All of a sudden, I heard someone shout, "Medication!" It was a worker in the office. This was a call for all residents to come over to the office door, stand in line and take their medication. **Page 86**

Psychosocial Interventions. Geneva receives this type of treatment through the boarding home where she lives and the mental health treatment center where she attends daily. Between the two programs, she is able to manage her mental illness and live somewhat of an independent lifestyle. Read and discuss the excerpts below.

She explained to me that Geneva resided in an assisted living facility, in which they cook, clean, wash clothes, and manage medication for the residents. **Page 20**

The work of the center includes evaluating mental health patients, setting behavior goals, creating treatment plans and providing therapeutic activities. While there, Mother participates with group counseling, games and trips to the park. She also receives lunch and a snack and learns life skills. **Page 21**

Overall, I was impressed with the work of the boarding home and mental health treatment center. I realized they are committed to that specific community of people. They have taken on the challenge of providing their basic physical, emotional and mental health needs. **Page 115**

Psychosocial Intervention: Social Support. During the author's second trip to visit Geneva, the mental health treatment center allowed her to sit in the lobby and talk with the author in lieu of center activities. Read and discuss the excerpt below.

For a moment, I was feeling a little guilt, like we were causing her to miss the center activities. Then I realized the staff probably felt like visiting with her long-lost family may be more therapeutic to her than participating with the center for that day. **Page 56**

Mental Hospital. During times when symptoms are severe, patients may be hospitalized to help relieve symptoms. The author's story indicates that Geneva has been a mental hospital patient numerous times throughout her life. Read and discuss the excerpts below.

Donna said she had to remind my mother that if she did not take her medication that she could end up locked up in a mental hospital again. Having a fear of going back there, she started taking it regularly. **Page 55**

However, if she refuses to take it, her uncontrollable behavior places her at risk of being committed, against her will, to a mental hospital. **Page 76**

From her story, coupled with things I already knew, I gathered that she had already been in and out of mental facilities several times before I was even born." **Page 101**

It was in Kansas City where she experienced her final mental hospital stay before leaving our family for good. **Page 102**

They told me it was a regular hospital, that would help my body rejuvenate and give me some rest from the kids. After they admitted me, I found out it was a mental hospital. **Page 102**

She recalled being in the mental hospital and no one ever coming to see her. 'He stayed away. **Page 103**

She alleged, "There is a lot I don't know. I did not have a chance to talk to my husband before I left the mental hospital with a friend. **Page 104**

"Were you in a mental hospital at the time of my birth?" She said, "Yes." **Page 108**

Effects on the author

Feeling Emotional. After the very emotional reunion, the author needed to talk about her thoughts and feeling with someone who would listen to her, and not be judgmental. Read and discuss the excerpts below.

After a meticulous online search, I found the number of a counseling hotline where I could speak with someone freely without revealing my true identity[...]Realizing I finally had a golden opportunity to share what was on my heart concerning my mother, with someone who did not know me and therefore could not judge me, tears welled up in my eyes. I cried and began to talk about my feelings.
Page 13-14

These ***Further Discussion Points*** are only a few things that stood out for the author from her own story. Did you see any additional Symptoms, Coping Behaviors, Treatments or Effects on the author as you read the book? If so, please free to discuss them.

FINDING MOTHER SERIES

A Gifted Child in Foster Care:
A Story Resilience – REVISED EDITION
In this book, Dr. Grace LaJoy shares her life story of being deserted by her mother, living in foster care, and ending up in a gifted and talented class while still in foster care. She recalls her life story before, during and after foster care. The *Finding Mother Series* was written as a sequel to this book.

Finding Mother After Five Decades:
A Story of Hope
Grace LaJoy's determination pays off when she finally finds her mother who abandoned her at age two. Discover the specific details about her intriguing journey in **Finding Mother after Five Decades,** BOOK 1 of the *Finding Mother Series.*

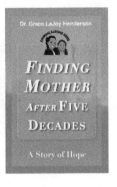

Reuniting with Mother:
A Story of Tenacity
What happens when Grace LaJoy and her siblings come face-to-face with their estranged mother after 49 years? How does she receive them? Find out in **Reuniting with Mother,** BOOK 2 of the *Finding Mother Series*.

AFTER THE REUNION: A STORY OF ACCEPTANCE
Grace LaJoy Henderson

After the Reunion:
A Story of Acceptance
After a very emotional reunion, Grace LaJoy has two concerns to address with her long-lost mother. What are her concerns? Does she get the answers she needs from her mother? Find out in **After the Reunion,** BOOK 3 of the *Finding Mother Series.*

Diary of Emotion:
Thoughts and Feelings
After reuniting with her mother after 49 years, Grace LaJoy toils with an array of thoughts and feeling. She reveals them all in **Diary of Emotions,** BOOK 4 of the *Finding Mother Series.*

Available in softcover and Kindle eBook
Collect them all at Amazon.com
Ask for the series in
bookstores and libraries
www.gracelajoy.com

PRAISES FOR THE
FINDING MOTHER SERIES

Grace LaJoy Henderson's *Finding Mother Series* is a revelation. It is a gift to discover an author who can write so honestly—and with such vulnerability—about the joy and pain of reuniting with a parent after a 49-year separation. Henderson never glosses over the frightening or disappointing parts of her story. But her compassionate, unwavering voice, as she uncovers the long arc of her mother's life, is itself a triumph. **~Whitney Terrell, Associate Professor of English, University of Missouri-Kansas City**

"The author's emotional honesty and the balancing of positive and negative emotions is what makes this series work." **~Phoebe Shanahan, MA in English Literature**

"The Finding Mother Series will inspire readers to *feel* their feelings. It stirs people in similar situations to be at peace, but at the same time seek growth, in the midst of their circumstances." **Arica Miller, LMSW, School Social Worker**

"The *Finding Mother Series* displays a perfect example of how one triggering event can cause conflicting emotions. Throughout the series, the author experienced hope *and* despair, excitement *and* apprehension. Two, totally opposite emotions both at the same time. However, both were completely justified! This range and transition of emotions is what drives the entire *series*. Secondary students will absolutely benefit from reading this collection of books." **~Jacob Kelow, M.S.Ed., Secondary School Counselor, Kansas City Public Schools**

PRAISES continued →

"The *Finding Mother Series* is written in a very powerful, real and authentic voice style. The author's honesty shines through her writing. Although the author's sadness throughout the story is quite palpable, her attitude towards her mentally ill mother is full of grace and understanding despite the fact that she had abandoned her. This is a clear and honest work." **~Fay Collins, Writer-Editor**

"The *Finding Mother Series* is a beautiful sequence of books. The author's reunion with her mother is very well documented." **~Phyllis Harris, Former Missouri State Director, Parent Information Resource Center**

"The author shares her personal story in an authentic way. Easy reading. Flows well." **~Ila Barrett, Behavioral Therapist, Jacksonville, FL**

"The Finding Mother Series is an inspiration to all who have faced abandonment by a parent. Grace LaJoy's truth validates her determination never to extinguish the fire, which burned in her soul to find her mother." **~ Dr. Gwendolyn Squires, Former School Principal, Kansas City Public Schools**

"Reading this series may help others who long to be reunited with their parents." **~Dr. Mary E. McConnell, Educator, University of Missouri-Kansas City**

"The Finding Mother Series will touch many people who are in this same situation, but who may not have the forgiveness in their hearts that the author and her siblings have. It is going to touch lives in more ways than you can imagine." **~Jean Smith, Dallas, TX**

"I strongly believe that this series will heal a lot of broken hearts and act as a source of encourage, advice, guidance and counsel for people in such scenarios; both children and adults." **~Ken J.**

ABOUT THE AUTHOR

Dr. Grace LaJoy Henderson
is the author of over thirty books. Her foster care story, *A Gifted Child in Foster Care: A Story of Resilience, Classroom Set* and her children's book series, *The Gracie Series*, are currently being used in public and charter schools.

Pearson Higher Education published two chapters from her foster care story in a college textbook.

She has earned a Doctorate in Christian Counseling, a Master's of Education in Guidance and Counseling, and a Master of Arts in Curriculum and Instruction. She has also earned a Bachelor's degree in Social Psychology.

Dr. Henderson managed a contract with the Missouri Children's Division, in which she provided court ordered mentoring for foster youth, supervised parent-child visits and parent education. She has served as psychology and college success instructor as well as academic coach. Outside of higher education, she is a keynote speaker, workshop leader and guest author at schools, libraries and other organizations. Newspapers, radio and television has featured her publications and her story.

AFTER THE REUNION: A STORY OF ACCEPTANCE
Grace LaJoy Henderson